jamie's italy

JAMIE OLIVER
jamie's italy

photographs by david loftus
and chris terry

HYPERION

NEW YORK

I dedicate this book to some amazing people who have helped me fall in love with Italy: Gennaro Contaldo, Rose Gray, Ruth Rogers, David Gleave, Theo Randall, Patricia Michelson, and Elizabeth David

Published by arrangement with Michael Joseph / The Penguin Group
Copyright © 2006 Jamie Oliver
Photographs copyright © David Loftus 2006
Additional photographs by Chris Terry and Peter Begg copyright © 2006

Library of Congress Cataloging-in-Publication Data has been applied for.
ISBN 1-4013-0195-9

Hyperion books are available for special promotions and premiums.
For details contact Michael Rentas, Assistant Director, Inventory Operations,
Hyperion, 77 West 66th Street, 12th floor, New York, New York 10023, or call 212-456-0133.

FIRST EDITION

10 9 8 7 6 5 4 3 2 1

contents

ciao! tutto bene?

Since I was a teenager I've been totally besotted by the love, passion and verve for food, family and life itself that just about all Italian people have, no matter where they're from or how rich or poor they might be. And that is what I'm passionate about – good food for everyone, no matter what. Many Italians never say they are from Italy. Instead they are from Venice or Sicily or Naples, and this is the whole point – their regionality is so exciting. But I've also learned on my journey around Italy that the word regional, when it comes to cooking, is the tip of the iceberg. They are far more parochial than that. There should be a word invented for it like "villagional," because these guys, rightly or wrongly, will argue that their own village makes a certain thing in the most perfect way and will look down on another village's method with utter contempt! The only other thing I've witnessed which brings out such emotion in people is football.

It's this passion that is reflected in their food. They'll spend ages arguing about where the best stew is from, or the best pappardelle, or olive oil, or seafood. If you've ever seen one of these heated exchanges, you'll know they're not being aggressive – they're simply arguing their point! I love the fact that they think their own regional way of cooking is the best, and how they are so proud of their local produce, and how every Italian loves to talk about food. Even though I don't speak a whole lot of Italian, I didn't once find it a problem trying to have conversations about food and recipes – it's a universal thing!

But the thing I love most about the Italians is that somehow, although they have some of the best fashion designers and cars in the world, they've managed to retain a unique sense of tradition and village spirit. Right now in villages around Italy you'll still see people swapping cheese for some preserved vegetables, or the local old boy's rocket-fuel grappa for some equally mind-blowing mostarda di Cremona (mustard fruit pickle). I also find it quite incredible that traditions and festivals celebrating food happen weekly, monthly, yearly, anywhere from large town squares to the smallest gatherings in the most unpopulated parts of Italy.

It was only about 150 years ago that Italy was truly unified from twenty-seven different states into one country, thanks to good old Garibaldi. This is why there is such diversity in lifestyles, cooking, traditions, and dialects. And this is why as a chef I find the country so damn exciting. I mean, just how many ways can you shape a bit of flour, water, and eggs into pasta? Genius! And you know what? I should have been bloody Italian – why, oh why, was I born in Southend-on-Sea? No disrespect to my roots, of course!

The truth is, when I'm in Italy I feel Italian – even with my very basic grasp of the language I manage to get by, and you know why? Because, like all Italians, I love my family for better or for worse and because food has been something I've grown up around. If you are at the market and you ask the fruit man if you can taste one of his beautiful grapes, he will immediately recognize you as someone who cares and will give you respect. When I found myself at a vegetable stand in a small village in Tuscany, being served by a disheveled old bloke, I told him I was going to be cooking for some grape-pickers and he questioned me straight away, saying it was far too early to be picking the grapes because "The Sangiovese is not ready yet." My friends had just finished picking a less common Merlot which was ready to go – but how many countries can you go to where the local vegetable stand holder has such intricate knowledge of local produce? Amazing! On another occasion I was cooking a birthday meal for an Italian family in Puglia and I asked the six-year-old daughter, in my bad Italian, what meat she would like – well, first of all I said *"cane"* instead of *"carne,"* so we didn't get off to a great start, because she thought I was asking how I should cook her dog! So after that mix-up she asked for beef. As I walked off she called after me and asked what piece I was going to cook. She then stipulated a rib steak (similar to a T-bone), the cut she felt was the most delicious piece of the animal. And then, knock me down, she informed me that I was allowed to use rosemary on the grilled beef, but only rosemary because that's the way it was in Puglia! Rosemary could only be used on roasted chicken and grilled beef. Period. Coming from such a young child, this completely surprised me.

And when I was in Bari, also in Puglia, I met another young girl who made orecchiette, cappelletti, and fusilli pasta faster and more accurately than any chef I've met in my life! I fell in love with this seven-year-old, not just because she was beautiful and lovely but because she was such a genius pasta-maker and she taught me how to make a few pastas I've never made by hand before. She sat on one side of me and her eighty-eight-year-old great-grandma was on the other side – this lady had been making pasta every single day of her life since she was four.

In writing this book, I didn't just want to give you a collection of Italian recipes. I wanted to share some great experiences with you at the same time. So I wrote it while I traveled around the country, working and eating and meeting people off the beaten track. I wanted to find the food of the "real" Italy – not the place that conjures up images of olive groves and lemons – and to celebrate the recipes from the people I met along the way, from fishermen to family bakers, from the street full of mamas making fresh pasta to all those taking part in the local pasta competition in the town square. I wanted to experience for myself the spirit of Italy that makes cooking and eating absolutely central to family life, whichever part of the country you find yourself in.

And I want you to experience it too. I want you to walk past the wall of footballing posters in Palermo and chuckle because you've seen it here. I want you to go and find the old woman making polenta in the town of Bari in Puglia. Or go and visit the lovely people who run the Petrolo estate in Tuscany, or the family-run Agriturismo La Grotta dei Folletti in Le Marche. I want you to go and see Dario the butcher in Panzano in Chianti and shake his hand. Tell him you're a friend of mine and ask him if you can try his sushi del Chianti. I want you to buy twelve artichokes from the weathered old codger in the market in Rome who picks and prepares and removes the chokes so quickly that it would make the most highly decorated Michelin-star chef in the world look like an amateur, and then I want you to go home and cook two recipes using artichokes. I don't want to get too deep, but when you start enjoying food with lovely people in different places on different occasions you end up with meaningful snapshots that you'll remember forever. This is how it works for me, anyway!

One of the reasons I went to Italy on this trip was to learn, but I also wanted to try to get a feel for why the country has retained its amazing food culture. I have my own opinion – I think it's partly because it has great weather and resources for making great food; it's also down to traditions and family values and, I think, in some shape or form, religion and the Catholic Church, as any excuse for a festival or a gathering has an impact. But I think the main reason comes down to lack of choice. In the countryside, especially, the working class definitely don't have the same kind of choices that people in many other parts of the world have.

I've witnessed so many young people and teenagers in Italy living a "modern-day life" that we would have seen in Britain or the U.S. seventy years ago – yes, they have cell phones and computers but they're not seen as an essential part of everyday life and not as many people have them as here. There is also a massive working-class population and a very small proportion of wealthy people.

So I think Italy has managed to retain a lot of its brilliant things because there hasn't been a lot of choice available. I really believe that. And for me it creates quite a profound emotion because sometimes when you have too much choice you can lose sight of the things that really matter – your family, your kids, and your health. With Italians being the third longest-living nation in the world, behind the Japanese and the Icelanders, you can see that they're not doing much wrong, even with a lack of choice! Yes, they do eat loads of saturated fat and olive oil, and they also cook on charcoal and wood (which is supposed to be carcinogenic), but they eat in a balanced way – loads of fruit, veg, fish, and meat – and they keep active.

Undertaking manual labor, like olive-picking, to an old age is very common. In Tuscany some of the best olive oil producers still pay their workers in olive oil, not cash. For four to six weeks of the year olives are picked and many families give up their time to do this hard manual labor. A good olive-picker can pick up to ninety or one hundred kilos a day, and depending on how much oil the olives give (this is obviously dependent on the weather conditions each year) the pickers can receive around five to six liters of oil a day for their work. Can you imagine someone from Britain or the U.S.

doing this amount of hard work for that? Mind you, the workers love it because the government can't tax them on it and it gives them olive oil for their families for a whole year.

Italy has now become incredibly easy and cheap to get to, and this means many more of us can now go there. My best advice is to get out of the touristy places and into the real Italy, where good food and wine do not cost much. If you go to tourist spots, you may well get ripped off. If you use some basic Italian phrases, put a smile on your face, have enthusiasm for food and a twinkle in your eye, you can pretty much guarantee that you'll be looked after by the Italians.

Unless you're going somewhere like the Amalfi coast in order to sunbathe and swim in the sea, it's best to rent a car and drive around from one *agriturismo* to another. A few hours' research in the guidebooks will put together an incredible route. As a foreigner to Italy, and as someone who's interested in food, the one thing you've got on your side that the Italians are sometimes not so good at is being incredibly open-minded. Even though it's one of my favorite countries in the world (and one day I hope to live there), I sometimes find it incredibly frustrating that Italians can be stubborn and not want to try a dish or a different combination of flavors because it's not from their village or region, or it's not the way their mama would do it. I just think that life is too short not to try things – no matter how good your own way might be, you're not always going to be right. So my advice when you're traveling to Italy is to stay open-minded and you'll be blown away by the experience. Just get out there and enjoy yourself!

mun

Alimento Solido

OCIETÀ DEL PLASMON
MILANO

antipasti
starters

antipasti

Antipasti are served throughout Italy, but the content differs totally from region to region. In the north you'll get an incredible selection of cured meats, like bresaola, prosciutto, coppa di parma, and salamis of all shapes and sizes. But in the south you're more likely to be served marinated octopus or sardines or raw anchovies. Like pasta and bread, antipasti are a real signpost for regionality in Italy. Generally they are always served at room temperature. In restaurants and trattorias your drinks will arrive at the table followed first by some olives, then maybe by some sliced meats. As a chef you have to be extremely organized to get everything on the table at once, but in Italy it's *tranquillo* and you can take your time, as it's expected that little bowls and plates will arrive in flurries.

Probably more than any other menu course in Italy, antipasti can change and adapt to whatever's in season. Take fava beans, for example. They might be boiled and dressed with a little oil and lemon, or mashed up with a little pecorino, mint, lemon juice, and good oil. I've seen them served from their pods on a plate with a lump of pecorino, or boiled, smashed, and folded into a batter to be eaten as a hot fritto. Or they can be mixed with leftover risotto rice and deep-fried . . . As long as it tastes nice and reflects the season it's an antipasto.

In a lot of the places where I've eaten incredible antipasti a really chintzy old-fashioned trolley with bowls and platters has been wheeled around the room and the antipasti decanted onto little plates for your table. Or there might just be some bowls of antipasti in the corner of the restaurant where the cutlery's kept! What I'm trying to say is, feel free to huddle up some plates in the corner of your kitchen and keep them there until your friends sit down, then simply move them to the table. Remember:

• Real cooks champion only local, seasonal, fresh produce.

• You need to think about the selection. If you're serving six or more dishes, it's important to offer, say, something pickled alongside something using fresh veg, something mushy alongside something quite chunky and robust. If most of the dishes are cold or at room temperature, the odd dish that's warm and crunchy, like a fritto misto or hot beans drizzled with good oil, really wakes up the senses. This, for me, is when antipasti get exciting.

• Each individual plate should have its own flavor. I'd avoid seasoning all the dishes with the same thing – be it balsamic or red wine vinegar, lemon juice, or herbs. One dish flavored with one of these things is great, but don't dress or flavor them all the same way. Think of each dish as a different experience, and if you can do that you'll be making as good an antipasti selection as anyone.

This chapter embraces some of my favorite antipasti. Other books that have great antipasti are the *River Café* cookbooks by Rose Gray and Ruth Rogers, *Passione* by Gennaro Contaldo, the *Chez Panisse Café Cookbook* by Alice Waters, and *The Essentials of Classic Italian Cooking* by Marcella Hazan.

capitano vittorio –
a great farmer from
mercatello in
le marche

bruschette
large toasted bread

A bruschetta is a kind of open sandwich and it's probably where the idea for cheese on toast originally came from. It's normally made from a large loaf of sourdough natural yeast bread, which is a dark gray color and has a higher water content than usual in the dough. It also has a thick crust, and because of this, moisture is retained in the bread, meaning it can be used up to a week after purchasing. Have a look around a farmers' market or in a good supermarket and you should be able to find some. If you can't, a good-quality round country-style loaf will give you good results.

The bread is best sliced a half-inch thick and toasted on a grill, but it can also be done in a griddle pan for ease at home. After that it should be lightly rubbed a couple of times with a cut clove of garlic, then drizzled with some good extra virgin olive oil and sprinkled with salt and pepper. The toppings can be as humble or as luxurious as you like, from chopped herbs or a squashed tomato with basil, to marinated vegetables or beautiful cheeses, to lovely flaked crabmeat. The only rule is that whatever goes on top of a bruschetta should be nice and fresh and cooked with care. On the next page are my favorite toppings. They will each cover four to six slices.

basic bruschette

If you have a large loaf, cut it in half, then slice it crossways about a half-inch thick. Grill these slices on a grill or in a griddle pan until they are crisp on both sides, then lightly rub each piece a couple of times with a cut clove of garlic. Drizzle with some good extra virgin olive oil and sprinkle with a tiny pinch of salt. You can eat the toasted bread just like this, but make sure the oil is the best you can find, otherwise it will never taste good.

eggplant and mint

2 nice firm eggplants, the round purple
  Italian ones if possible, sliced
  lengthwise about ⅛ inch thick
extra virgin olive oil
white wine or herb vinegar
2 sprigs of fresh flat-leaf parsley, leaves
  picked and finely sliced

a small handful of fresh mint, leaves picked
  and finely sliced
1 clove of garlic, peeled and very
  finely sliced
sea salt and freshly ground black pepper

Heat a griddle pan until nice and hot. Lay your eggplant slices on it side by side, and when they are nicely charred on both sides, put them into a bowl. You will probably need to do this in several batches. While the eggplants are grilling, put 8 tablespoons of olive oil and 3 tablespoons of vinegar, with the parsley, mint, and garlic, into another bowl and season with salt and pepper. When the eggplants are all done, add them to the dressing and mix around, then check the seasoning again and divide onto the bruschette. Press the topping into the toast so all the lovely flavor gets sucked in!

baby artichokes

8 baby artichokes (prepared as on page 136)
4 cloves of garlic, skins left on
juice of 1 lemon

extra virgin olive oil
a handful of fresh mint, leaves picked
sea salt and freshly ground black pepper

Place your prepared artichokes in a pan with just enough water to cover them. Add the garlic cloves and a little squeeze of lemon juice and cook until the stalks are tender. Drain in a colander, then place the artichokes back into the empty pan with 2 or 3 tablespoons of olive oil and fry for 4 minutes to get a bit of color on them. When they're slightly golden, remove from the heat, squeeze in a little lemon juice, add the mint, and season carefully to taste. Remove 4 artichoke halves from the pan and put to one side, then mash all the rest in the pan, using a fork to squash the garlic out of the skins (throw the skins away). Smear across your basic bruschette, tearing one of the reserved artichoke halves over the top of each. PS, It's also really nice to add a handful of freshly grated Parmesan to the mashed-up artichokes.

mixed roasted vegetables

½ a bulb of fennel, tough outer leaves
  removed
½ a yellow pepper, seeds removed
1 red pepper, halved and seeds removed
½ a zucchini, halved lengthwise and seeds
  removed
1 teaspoon dried oregano

a handful of fresh mint, leaves picked and
  chopped
olive oil
sea salt and freshly ground black pepper
juice of ½ a lemon
herb vinegar

Preheat your oven to 425°F. Chop the fennel and peppers into 1 inch chunks and slice the zucchini. Toss the vegetables together with the oregano, mint, and a good glug of olive oil, season with salt and pepper, then place on a baking tray and roast in the preheated oven for about half an hour, until nicely golden. Remove and allow to cool, then very finely chop or pulse in a food processor until the mixture looks like a spreadable kind of salsa. Season again to taste, and add another drizzle of olive oil and a little lemon juice and herb vinegar to give it a kick. Smear across your basic bruschette.

tomato and basil

2 handfuls of nice mixed ripe tomatoes
a small bunch of fresh basil, leaves picked
sea salt and freshly ground black pepper

olive oil
good-quality white wine or herb vinegar

Make sure your tomatoes are really ripe when making this topping. Give them a wash, remove their cores, then carefully squeeze out the seeds and discard them. Place the tomatoes in a bowl, tear in the basil, season with salt and pepper, then toss with a good glug of olive oil and a good swig of vinegar to balance the flavors to your taste. You can serve the tomatoes either chunky or finely chopped, or you can scrunch them between your fingers before putting them on your basic bruschette – really tasty.

caponata

incredible sicilian eggplant stew

This is a fantastic dish from southern Italy that's eaten as a warm vegetable side dish or a cold antipasto. Sicilians are really proud that it's made with produce from their island. All the different methods of making it are more or less the same – the thing that makes it special, though, is the quality of the eggplants, tomatoes, and vinegar. Always try to get hold of nice firm eggplants with very few seeds – have a look down in your local market to see if you can find different colors. You could even ask your produce clerk to cut one open so you can check it out. Don't be tempted to cut the eggplant chunks too small or they will take on so much oil that they will become heavy. If this happens you don't get to admire the lovely creamy flavor and texture. I've eaten caponata that's been swimming in olive oil, but I much prefer mine to be less oily.

olive oil
2 nice large purple eggplants, cut into
 large chunks
1 heaping teaspoon dried oregano
sea salt and freshly ground black pepper
1 small red onion, peeled and finely
 chopped
2 cloves of garlic, peeled and finely sliced
a small bunch of fresh flat-leaf parsley,
 leaves picked and stems finely chopped

2 tablespoons salted capers, rinsed, soaked,
 and drained
a handful of green olives, pits removed
2–3 tablespoons best-quality herb vinegar
5 large ripe tomatoes, roughly chopped
optional: 2 tablespoons slivered almonds,
 lightly toasted

Get yourself a large pan, pour in a couple of glugs of olive oil, and place on the heat. Add your eggplant chunks and oregano, season with a little salt, and toss around so the eggplant is evenly coated by the oil. Cook on a high heat for around 4 or 5 minutes, giving the pan a shake every now and then. (Depending on the size of your pan you may need to cook the eggplant in batches.) When the eggplants are nice and golden on each side, add the onion, garlic, and parsley stems and continue cooking for another couple of minutes. Feel free to add a little more oil to the pan if you feel it's getting too dry. Throw in the drained capers and the olives and drizzle over the herb vinegar. When all the vinegar has evaporated, add the tomatoes and simmer for around 15 minutes or until tender. Taste before serving and season if you need to with salt, pepper, and a little more vinegar. Drizzle with some good olive oil and serve sprinkled with the chopped parsley leaves and the almonds if you like.

verdure verdi condite alla perfezione
dress up perfectly cooked greens

In Britain and the U.S. we tend not to eat enough veg, and when we do we always feel they need to be eaten with meat or fish. However, in Italy huge amounts of vegetables and greens are served as an antipasto just to get the tastebuds going. It's because of this that the Italians are a damn sight healthier than us. So listen up. Let's be like them and big up the greens. Cook them nicely, dress them with care and you'll be laughing.

So, first things first: get a large pot of salted boiling water on the go, with a lid on. If you're cooking Swiss chard, the stalks will need to be removed and added to the water first. When they've softened you can add the leaves, which need only a minute or two in boiling water. If you're cooking broccoli, or Romanesco broccoli, don't cook it al dente but don't overcook it either – you want it somewhere in between. How do you check? Take a piece out of the water and eat it. You can also use asparagus, or cabbage leaves like Savoy Napa, or cavolo nero, or zucchini. There are so many things that are green and lovely that can be cooked this way – just get into the spirit of it and see where it takes you.

Cook the greens with your full attention, then drain them well in a colander and lay them on a clean kitchen towel on a tray to soak up any excess moisture. Leave them for a few minutes to let the steam escape. While they're still warm I want you to dress them as you would a salad, with lemon juice and three times as much good extra virgin olive oil, and season carefully with salt and pepper to taste. Sometimes I put a few whole garlic cloves in the blanching water to soften them so I can mush them up and add them to the dressing.

Try to get into the habit of serving a small plate of greens like this for dinner as often as possible. I know it's a simple recipe but I think humans are so programmed to have certain things in certain situations, like meat with two veg, that I really want you to try stuff like this, done well, on its own, with a good drizzle of olive oil. How bloody good is that?

ricotta fritta con piccola insalata di pomodori

serves 6

fried ricotta with a little tomato salad

The nearest thing I can compare these little ricotta "cakes" to is really light gnocchi. When cooked, the cakes will be thin, crispy, and golden on the outside with a lovely, fluffy, silky ricotta inside. They are perfect with a little chopped tomato salad and can be eaten as a starter, a snack, or a hot canapé. I'm sure that once you've tried them you'll be making them all the time – they are incredibly quick and easy. What you need to do, though, is make sure that your family are all sitting around the table when you start to fry them (with cutlery and warmed plates ready) because these ricotta cakes taste so good when eaten straight away – it's worth being a bossy-boots at this point, they'll all thank you for it! PS, Buy your ricotta from a deli or specialty market as supermarket ricotta generally won't work.

1 lb. good crumbly ricotta cheese
2 tablespoons freshly grated Parmesan
  cheese, plus extra for serving
1½ tablespoons flour
sea salt and freshly ground black pepper
1 large egg, preferably organic
a large handful of mixed ripe tomatoes

2 sprigs of fresh basil
1 fresh red chili, deseeded and finely
  chopped
extra virgin olive oil
good red wine vinegar
olive oil
nutmeg, for serving

Mix the ricotta with the Parmesan, flour, a good pinch of salt, and the egg. Season with a little freshly ground black pepper and place in the fridge.

Halve the tomatoes, squeeze out the seeds, and discard them. Chop the flesh up into small chunks and drain off any excess liquid. Chop the stems of the basil finely and tear the leaves up roughly, then add to the tomatoes with the chili. Season with salt and pepper, a glug of good extra virgin olive oil, and a small swig of good red wine vinegar.

Put a nonstick pan on medium heat and add a splash of olive oil. Drop a few spoonfuls of the ricotta mix into the pan – make sure not to overcrowd it; the pieces shouldn't be touching. (Call the family to the table if you haven't done so already!) Fry the ricotta cakes for a couple of minutes or until golden brown, then carefully turn them over using a broad, flat knife or a fish server and fry them on the other side for a further minute.

Serve at once, with a light sprinkling of sea salt, a little nutmeg (grated from a height), and a good spoonful of the chopped tomatoes on the side. Drizzle over a little peppery extra virgin olive oil and grate over some Parmesan. Eat while crisp and warm!

sushi del chianti

serves 4

chianti sushi

Dario Ceccini is one of the best butchers in Italy. His little shop is in the town of Panzano in Chianti and it's usually packed with people eating and drinking the free food and wine that he gives out, especially on a Sunday morning at about ten o'clock – if you're lucky you may even get to hear him singing to his customers! From a business point of view, I've tried to work out how he has the time and the money to give all this stuff away, but it obviously works because he sells lots of produce.

When this "Chianti sushi" came out on a big platter with chopsticks hanging off the side of it for customers to use, I thought Dario must be taking me for a ride, but essentially it's a Tuscan version of a steak tartare. It's slightly fresher, really tasty, and the easiest thing in the world to make. However, I would only suggest having a go at it if you can get yourself some good-quality organic or free-range beef that's been hung for at least sixteen days. Don't use any old rubbish. As it's locally available to him, Dario was using the local Chianina white beef which is famous in that part of Tuscany. What was interesting was that he wasn't using the more predictable sirloin or rump, but instead was using top round. This cut would classically be used for making bresaola or salt beef, but check out his special way of making it tender in the method.

1 lb. 2 oz. best-quality beef top round
sea salt and freshly ground black pepper
1 small dried chili, crumbled
zest of 1 orange

a small handful of fresh sweet marjoram or
 a little less of fresh oregano, leaves picked
juice of 1 lemon
extra virgin olive oil

Your beef shouldn't have any sinews on it at all, but if it has, remove them with a knife, then slice and finely chop the meat. Now it's time to bash it up! If you have one of those hammer-type meat tenderizers, that's the best thing to use, or just get hold of something small and heavy. Spend a few minutes bashing the meat, until it looks a little bit like finely ground beef.

It was at this point that I noticed Dario sprinkled a good pinch of salt and pepper over the meat with the chili, half the orange zest, and most of the marjoram. He bashed it for another minute to really get the flavors in, so do this now! Next he chopped it for another 10 seconds or so, mixing it all up nicely and pulling it into the middle from the sides, tasted it for seasoning, and transferred it to a platter.

Once you have the meat spread out over your platter, squeeze the lemon juice over the top and drizzle with extra virgin olive oil. Scatter with the remaining marjoram leaves and orange zest before serving, and eat with chopsticks and bruschette.

riding around
the backstreets
of rome

fritto di salvia e alici

sage and anchovy fritters

In Italy you'll see these served as part of a fritto misto or as a nibble with a drink – they're a great thing to give your mates when they turn up at a party. It's a slightly unusual combination, but fried sage with anchovies is a brilliant mix. They will melt together and become fantastically meaty, almost like a steak. You may think I'm exaggerating here, but you have to try it!

A warning: You're going to be deep-fat frying, so if you have small children in the house when you're making these fritters, please, please, make sure the pan is out of reach ...

12 good-quality anchovy fillets
  in olive oil
a small glass of vin santo or sweet
  white wine, or the zest and juice
  of 1 lemon
24 large fresh sage leaves
flour, for dusting
sunflower oil

for the batter
2 cups bread flour
a pinch of salt
1 egg yolk, preferably organic
¾ cup water
⅓ cup fizzy mineral water
6 tablespoons olive oil
2 egg whites, preferably organic

First of all, place your anchovy fillets on a flat plate, pour over your vin santo, sweet wine, or lemon juice and zest, and leave to marinate for at least an hour. While this is happening, you can make your batter. Put the flour, salt, egg yolk, and water into a mixing bowl. Using a whisk, mix everything together until you have a thick custard consistency. Add the fizzy water a little at a time, then add the olive oil. Leave to stand for 30 minutes or so before using.

Moisten all the sage leaves with a sprinkling of water and dust both sides of them with a little flour. Take 2 sage leaves and put 1 on either side of an anchovy fillet so that you make a "sandwich." Squeeze together firmly so that a little moisture comes out of the anchovy.

Pour sunflower oil into a large sturdy saucepan or deep-fat fryer so it's at least 2 inches deep. Put it on a high heat until it reaches 350°F – if you're using a saucepan you will need to test it either with a cooking thermometer or, as I do, by dropping a small piece of potato into the oil. When the oil is at the right temperature the potato will turn golden. At this point turn the heat down to medium. While the oil is heating, whisk the egg whites with a pinch of salt until stiff, then slowly fold in the batter mixture until smooth. (You can use this batter for just about anything.) Have a plate standing by with a few sheets of paper towel on it.

Now you're ready to start fritto-ing! Pick up an anchovy sandwich and dip the whole thing into the batter, making sure it is coated thinly but well. Lightly wipe off any excess batter against the rim of the bowl, then carefully lower the sandwich into the pan of oil. It's best to fry about 6 at a time (obviously you can do more if you have a large pan). Fry for around a minute, until golden and crisp, then remove to the paper towels and serve right away before they go soggy.

antipasti | starters 19

limoni di amalfi cotti al forno

serves 4

amalfi baked lemons

Lemons are in such abundance on the Amalfi coast that you'd imagine the locals might be a bit fed up with them by the end of the summer! Coming up with some novel and tasty new ways to use their lemons is appreciated, so have a go at making this one. You don't actually eat the lemon skin; it's just there to flavor the mozzarella. It's obviously best to make this using amazing Amalfi lemons, but it does work equally well with large, unwaxed, preferably organic lemons instead. The finished thing is perfect as an antipasto or with an *aperitivo* to get your tastebuds going. I made about forty of these for my birthday dinner when I was in Minori and they went down really well.

2 large unwaxed lemons
1 or 2 5-oz. balls of buffalo mozzarella,
  sliced into ¼-inch-thick pieces
4 fresh basil leaves

2 anchovy fillets
2 ripe cherry tomatoes, halved
salt and freshly ground black pepper
optional: 1 dried red chili, crumbled

Preheat your oven to 400°F. Remove the ends of the lemons and discard them, then cut the lemons in half crossways, giving you 4 1-inch-thick discs. See the picture opposite to see what I mean. Now, using a small knife, remove the lemon flesh, leaving you with 4 hollow circles of skin. Basically, what we're going to do is flavor the mozzarella and push it inside the lemon skin so that it absorbs the lovely lemon flavor when it bakes.

Now, the mozzarella is obviously going to melt and ooze out when baked. In Italy, a lemon leaf is placed underneath each one to keep everything in place, but it's fine to use a square of waxed paper to do the same thing. So lay a waxed-paper square or a lemon leaf on a cutting board and place one of your lemon skin "wheels" on top. Cut a piece of mozzarella to fit inside, then lay a basil leaf, half an anchovy fillet, and half a cherry tomato on top with a small pinch of salt and pepper. Add a little dried chili if you like. Put another slice of mozzarella on top – the lemon skin should now be filled up. Do the same to the rest of the wheels, place them on a baking sheet, and cook in the preheated oven for 10 to 15 minutes, until golden and bubbling. Remove from the oven and allow to cool for a few minutes, then serve with some hot grilled crostini. Simply scoop the mozzarella out, eat with the toast, and mop up any juices. Delicious!

crostini

small toasted bread

I've always thought of crostini as small bruschette but this isn't completely correct, as they are usually made with white bread instead of sourdough. I'm told that in the old days the bread would have been so stale that it would have to be soaked in a little stock or juice to make it chewy and edible again, but don't worry. In this day and age you don't have to do this. In Italy they simply grill a half-inch slice of *ciabatta*, rub it with a cut clove of garlic, drizzle it with oil, and season it with salt and pepper. Crostini are a great *aperitivo* with a drink, especially if you offer a few different toppings. Here are a few of my faves to get you into the spirit of things—each one will make enough to top 12 slices of crostini.

1 loaf of ciabatta bread, cut into ½-inch slices
1 large clove of garlic, peeled and cut in half

good-quality extra virgin olive oil

Grill your slices of ciabatta. While they're still hot, rub them gently with the cut side of the garlic and drizzle with good-quality extra virgin olive oil. Finish with your favorite toppings . . .

prosciutto, figs, and mint

Get yourself 6 large ripe figs, 12 slices of prosciutto, and a small bunch of fresh mint. Tear the figs in half, then drape a piece of prosciutto over each of your hot crostini and squash a piece of fig on top. Finish with mint leaves and serve drizzled with a little extra virgin olive oil, a drop of balsamic vinegar, and some freshly ground black pepper.

greens

Take 3 large handfuls of cavolo nero, cabbage, or Swiss chard and strip the leaves off the stalks. Add 3 cloves of peeled garlic to a pan of salted water and bring to a boil, then add the greens. Cook until tender, then drain well in a colander and allow to cool. Squeeze out any excess water from the greens, mush up the garlic, season to taste with sea salt and freshly ground black pepper, and drizzle with extra virgin olive oil. Toss around and divide onto each of your hot crostini, drizzled with more olive oil and a squeeze of lemon juice.

buffalo mozzarella and chili

Tear 3 5-oz. balls of buffalo mozzarella into quarters, then top each of your hot crostini with one of the quarters. Deseed and finely chop a fresh red chili and sprinkle this over the mozzarella. Add a little seasoning and finish with a drizzle of extra virgin olive oil. Lovely with a little fresh basil torn over.

pea and fava bean purée with pecorino

In a mortar and pestle or a food processor, smash up a small handful of mint leaves with 2 good handfuls of freshly shelled peas and fava beans until they look like mushy peas. Add a large handful of freshly grated pecorino or Parmesan, then loosen with a couple of good glugs of extra virgin olive oil and balance the flavors with a little lemon juice, salt, and pepper. Smear this over each of your hot crostini and finish with some grated pecorino or Parmesan and a little mint – genius!

mixed herbs

Get any mixture of soft herbs like fennel tops, green or purple basil, parsley, mint, chervil, thyme leaves, or sorrel and roughly chop them. Take 6 cherry tomatoes and halve them, then rub one of the halves into each of your hot crostini. Grate some pecorino or Parmesan over the top and season with salt and pepper. Drizzle with olive oil and sprinkle over your chopped herbs.

squashed cannellini beans with garlic

Pick the leaves off a couple of sprigs of rosemary and pound them gently in a mortar and pestle with a little salt. Add a glug of extra virgin olive oil and stir, then put to one side. Fry 2 sliced cloves of garlic in a little olive oil until lightly golden. Add 1¾ cups of good-quality drained and rinsed cannellini beans and continue to simmer gently for 7 minutes. Season the beans well with salt and pepper and a swig of red wine vinegar, then mash them up using the back of a fork until you have a coarse purée. Smear your hot crostini with the bean purée and spoon your rosemary oil over the top.

tomatoes and olives

Get yourself about 20 ripe cherry tomatoes, different colors if possible, and cut them into quarters. Remove the pits from a handful of good-quality black or green olives and chop them up. Toss in a bowl with the tomatoes, 2 or 3 glugs of extra virgin olive oil, and a swig of balsamic vinegar and season carefully with salt and pepper and a little crumbled dried chili. (Some olives are salty, so go easy.) Spoon over each of your hot crostini and sprinkle some baby basil leaves over the top.

funghi al forno ripieni di ricotta serves 4

baked mushrooms stuffed with ricotta

This is an incredible version of the old classic we've all tried at some point. You can use one type of mushroom or a mixture, but you will need ones which have a good cap to hold the ricotta filling. Small portobello, cremini, or field mushrooms will work well. You can serve this as a starter or as little antipasti munchies.

3½ oz. good crumbly ricotta cheese
zest of 1 lemon
1 fresh red chili, deseeded and finely
  chopped (to taste)
sea salt and freshly ground black pepper
2 tablespoons finely chopped fresh
  oregano or marjoram leaves

a good handful of freshly grated Parmesan
  cheese, plus extra for sprinkling
4 handfuls of mushrooms, brushed clean
extra virgin olive oil
a handful of arugula or soft leafy herbs

Preheat your oven to 425°F. Put your ricotta into a bowl with the lemon zest, chili, and a little salt and pepper. Beat together with a wooden spoon, then fold in your chopped oregano or marjoram and the Parmesan.

Carefully remove the stalks from your mushrooms and discard them (or keep them for making a pasta sauce), then toss the mushroom caps in a little oil, salt, and pepper. Lay them upside down on a baking sheet so that they can be filled with small amounts of your fantastic ricotta mixture. Carefully spoon in the filling, sprinkle a little Parmesan over the top, and bake in the preheated oven till golden – about 15 minutes. Great served on a big plate, sprinkled with some dressed arugula leaves or soft leafy herbs.

funghi tagliati a fettine sottili, con mozzarella fusa e timo

serves 4

sliced mushrooms with melted mozzarella and thyme

This is a great little recipe – it takes no time at all to put together and is perfect for serving at a party. I've used mozzarella, but another Italian cheese called scamorza would be good too. As this dish grills very quickly, I actually cook it on the plate I'm serving it on, but if you're using bone china, think again. (I don't want any bills through the post!)

2 big handfuls of mushrooms, very
  thinly sliced
2 5-oz. balls of mozzarella or scamorza
  cheese, torn into small pieces

a small sprig of fresh thyme, leaves picked
sea salt and freshly ground black pepper
extra virgin olive oil

Get yourself a large ovenproof platter and spread your mushrooms on it in one layer. Scatter over the cheese and the thyme leaves. Season with salt and pepper, drizzle with olive oil, and place the plate under the grill.

Grill for a couple of minutes, checking frequently, until the cheese is melted, bubbling, and golden, and tuck in! Serve with some crusty bread.

street food
& pizza

street food & pizza

I'm really excited about this chapter because street food is something not many books and cooks have focused on. The thing I love about it is its complete arrogance toward any rules or regulations! Most of the good street food I've eaten around Naples or in Sicily, especially in Palermo, comes from regular roadside vans offering porchetta sandwiches. Most of these vans, if opened up in England, would be shut down within a day because of EU health and hygiene regulations – well, I thought Italy, France, and Spain were in the EU, too, and it doesn't seem to stop them in the slightest! As far as the locals, or the policemen, are concerned, this street food has been prepared and sold in the same way for hundreds of years and they'll be damned if a geezer in Brussels is going to tell them to stop. They'd only open up again further down the road!

Years ago in England there was a really good street food culture, and today, even though the sausages and burgers are like donkey meat and full of crap, the smell of sweet onions as you enter a football stadium always gets the senses going. And the smell of chips with malt vinegar is always a winner. At Christmas, the tramps around London that light up charcoal fires and toast chestnuts for you, sprinkled with a little salt, are just brilliant. These guys peel chestnuts quicker than any chef I've ever met, and yes, they might have dirty hands, but bloody hell, the chestnuts taste good!

Now, I've got to be honest here ... about 50 percent of the street food I came across in Italy is pretty dodgy stuff! One old chap in an alleyway in Palermo was surrounded by about ten people all eating and talking. He had a big cauldron in his stall, with a double-lined tablecloth tied on top like a steamed pudding at Xmas. There was nothing similar about the contents, though ... This chain-smoking, dirty-looking bloke would put his hand into the cauldron through a small hole in the cover and draw out a handful of greasy gizzards, spleen, and lung which he would slap into a simple bread roll, or just serve on a bit of paper. Most of the people eating at the stall while I was there looked reasonably working-class and poor, but there was also the odd guy in a tweed jacket and cashmere rollneck wearing huge Prada goggles who would get off his scooter and have some of this old-school Italian street food.

Now, I've probably put you off this section of the book already, but the exciting thing is that the rest of the street food I came across, and have included here, even though it was served in very basic ways, is damn tasty. It certainly put a smile on my face, so I hope it does the same for you! This chapter includes recipes for a whole handful of those things, from Tuscan porchetta, to Sicilian chickpea fritters, to the most famous street food of them all ... pizza!

polenta fritta croccante con rosmarino e sale

fried crispy polenta with rosemary and salt

In village streets and markets around Italy you'll very often see little trailers with heated glass serving areas selling a whole bunch of fritto misto (deep-fried vegetables). These are lovely, but sometimes I've also been lucky enough to find a street vendor selling fried polenta – this isn't usually included as part of a fritto misto but it's a real joy. The nearest thing I can liken it to is a french fry, but polenta is slightly less absorbent of the oil and the Parmesan gives it a really nice rich flavor. In the past I've also added things like chopped chili, different herbs like oregano or marjoram, even fennel seeds or sun-dried tomatoes. None of the latter additions are particularly classic or authentic, but the results were very good. Whether you have it as munchies or tossed in a nice salad, or even serve it instead of fries, fried polenta is really tasty – so give it a shot.

A warning: when you fry with oil like this, it's really important not to try to do other jobs at the same time. Stay focused on the pan and keep any kids away from it.

1 firm polenta recipe (see page 269)
a handful of freshly grated Parmesan cheese
sea salt and freshly ground black pepper
2 handfuls of uncooked polenta
  for dusting

3½ pints sunflower oil, for frying
a handful of fresh rosemary, leaves picked

First, make your polenta – when you remove it from the heat, stir in the Parmesan and season to taste. Spread it out on an oiled tray or work surface until it's 1 inch thick – when it has cooled down and set, tear or cut it into large thumb-sized pieces. As far as I'm concerned, the rougher the better! Dust all the pieces with the uncooked polenta, as this will give them a nice crunch when fried.

Place a deep pan on a high heat and add the sunflower oil. Put a piece of potato into the oil – when it's frying good and fast, the oil will be at the perfect temperature. If you have a cooking thermometer, use that – you want the oil to be 350°F. If it gets too hot and starts smoking, use your common sense and turn the heat down. Put a handful of polenta into a small sieve and carefully lower the pieces into the oil – if they sink and nothing seems to be happening, you need more heat. If they're frying nicely, Bob's your uncle! After 4 minutes the polenta should be crispy and cooked. Now, I haven't seen this done in Italy but I like to add a handful of picked rosemary to the oil for the last 20 seconds of cooking – this gives incredible flavor and crunch. Carefully remove the polenta and rosemary with your sieve or a slotted spoon and put them on some paper towels. Dust with sea salt and serve immediately to your guests as pre-dinner nibbles or in a bowl as an accompaniment.

frittelle di spaghetti

makes 4

spaghetti fritters

I've seen fried pasta dishes before, but never thought all that much about them until I saw Giovanni, who runs a restaurant on the island of Marettimo, just off the coast of Sicily, fry me a spaghetti fritter and serve it in a very unusual way. He put it in a bowl with some broth and boiled pork from a bollito misto. Absolutely amazing. The broth made it go soggy but it was still beautiful to eat. But the great thing about fried pasta is its portability. It can also be eaten as antipasti or baked as an *al forno* dish (see page 114). And it's lovely for brunch. Once you've got the base recipe you can vary the flavor in different ways. For instance, I'm totally obsessed by chili, so I always add that to mine. Basically you bind the pasta with a little egg and season it with key Italian ingredients like parsley and Parmesan (but don't be tempted to use pre-grated Parmesan – it will taste horrible). From there you can add little flakes of fish, a sprinkling of chili, or little chopped-up tomatoes or olives. When it's cooked, the fritter should be soft in the middle and crunchy on the outside – fandabidozi!

2 cloves of garlic, peeled and finely chopped
a handful of fresh flat-leaf parsley,
  finely chopped
2 eggs, preferably organic
1 egg yolk, preferably organic
2 handfuls of freshly grated Parmesan cheese

optional: 2 anchovies, roughly chopped
1–2 dried chilies (to your taste), crumbled
sea salt and freshly ground black pepper
7 oz. dried pasta
olive oil

Put all your ingredients, apart from the spaghetti and olive oil, into a bowl and mix together. Add your spaghetti to a pan of salted, boiling water and cook according to the package instructions. Drain the pasta in a colander and rinse under cold water to cool it down. Once the pasta is cool, snip it with scissors into pieces roughly 3 inches long and add them to the bowl. Mix everything together well.

Pour a little oil into a pan and place on the heat. Then, using a fork, add piles (as big or as small as you like) of the spaghetti mixture to the pan and fry until golden and crisp on both sides. Sometimes it's delicious to fry the fritters in a slightly hotter pan so they become really golden on the outside but are a bit softer and warm inside.

insalata di strada

street salad

In Palermo there's a night market called Il Borgo, where all the locals gather to eat at little stalls selling things like chickpea fritters, boiled baby octopus, and some stuff that you wouldn't want to eat, like gizzards, spleen, and other dirty wobbly things! A lot of the veg stalls have massive cauldrons of boiled potatoes and artichokes to serve to their customers – I guess you could say this is the original fast food – and they taste absolutely brilliant.

Some of the stalls also make a version of this salad, which is delicious. They tend to dress it and have it hanging around for quite some time so it becomes a bit sloppy and past its best, but the principle of the salad is fantastic and all the locals absolutely adore it. In Sicily you can get these terrific Cedro lemons which are mainly pith and they are amazing in salads – but you may not be able to get hold of them. In this case I wouldn't recommend you use normal lemons as the flavor is quite different.

about 1 lb. new potatoes, scrubbed
sea salt and freshly ground black pepper
3 handfuls of mixed crunchy salad leaves,
  e.g. radicchio, arugula, romaine
a small handful of fresh mint leaves,
  picked and torn
1 bulb of fennel, halved and finely sliced,
  herby tops reserved
optional: ½ a Cedro lemon, sliced
  wafer thin

for the Sicilian blood orange dressing
juice of 1 blood orange
3 tablespoons good-quality white wine
  vinegar or herb vinegar
extra virgin olive oil
a good pinch of dried oregano
2 tablespoons capers, washed if using salted,
  chopped if large
sea salt and freshly ground black pepper

The way potatoes are cooked in Sicily is very long and very slow, on a low simmer with plenty of salt in the water. This is a fantastic method of making normal potatoes soft and floury, but in the case of new potatoes it would be a crime. So add them to fast-boiling salted water, as this will help retain a lot of their flavor, and cook them till nice and tender. The softer you can get them while still holding their shape, the better. While the potatoes are cooking, wash all your salad leaves and put them into a nice big bowl with the mint and fennel. If using a Cedro lemon, add the slices to the salad at this point.

For the dressing, mix the orange juice and vinegar in a glass jar or bowl with about twice as much extra virgin olive oil. Add the oregano and capers and season to taste with salt and pepper. Give it a good mix and have a taste. Don't forget that you want the flavor to be a little over the top, so that by the time you've dressed the salad with it and it has mixed with all the other flavors it's perfect because it's become more subtle. Drain the potatoes when cooked, and allow them to steam in a colander for 5 minutes. Throw them into the salad while still warm and toss together well. Absolutely fantastic – great with a plate of grilled fish or as a lunchie salad on its own.

panelle

chickpea fritters

The process of making these fritters is hardly any different from making polenta for grilling or frying (see page 269), it's just that you use chickpea flour instead of ground corn. The only other slight difference is that you should whisk the flour into the water before heating it, as this helps to stop lumps from forming. In Britain and the U.S. we think of flour as being made from wheat, but it can actually be made out of all sorts of things like rice, chickpeas, or chestnuts. Going back in history a couple of hundred years, particular areas in which people lived might have only been suitable for growing a few native things, like chickpeas for instance. And if this area was bordered by mountains or the sea, then you'd basically get stuck with the same small handful of ingredients for the rest of your life, and you'd probably get fed up and bored with them. To beat the monotony you would need to have been resourceful – chickpeas would have been turned into sweet things or pastas or flours. You can buy chickpea flour in some supermarkets and Asian food shops, where it's sometimes called gram flour.

1½ pints cold water
8oz chickpea flour
sea salt and freshly ground black pepper

a handful of fresh rosemary, sage, and oregano, finely chopped
3½ pints vegetable oil, for frying

Pour the water into a mixing bowl and sprinkle a little of the flour over the surface. Whisk it in and add a little more. Keep adding the flour in small amounts until it's all used up and whisked in, then season well with salt and pepper.

Pour the batter into a deep heavy-bottomed saucepan and place on a medium heat. Bring to a boil, whisking almost constantly, then turn the heat down to a simmer. The batter should thicken, so change from a whisk to a wooden spoon and keep stirring, making sure you get into all the corners. Taste the thickened batter – it should taste slightly bitter, a bit like peanuts from the shell. Keep cooking and stirring for about 5 minutes or so until this taste has gone.

Working quickly before the batter sets, season again with salt and pepper if you need to, stir in the chopped herbs and pour it out onto lightly oiled plates. Spread it out with a spatula until it's about ¼-inch thick and leave to cool.

Place a deep, sturdy, heavy-bottomed pan on a high heat and add the oil. Put a piece of potato into the oil – when it's frying good and fast, the oil will be at the perfect temperature. If you have a cooking thermometer, use that – you want the oil to be 350°F. If it gets too hot and starts smoking, use your common sense and turn the heat down. Score or tear the batter into triangle-ish shapes, then gently peel them off the plates and very carefully place them into the hot oil a few at a time. Fry for a minute or two, until lightly golden, then remove with a slotted spoon and drain on paper towels. When you have enough, sprinkle with a little salt and serve.

the sicilian grillers at the
il borgo night market

il pesce fritto in pastella all'italiana più croccante

italian style fish with the crispiest batter

I went to a fantastic shop in Rome that was selling salt cod in batter. In Rome they tend to use salt cod, which is a fillet of cod that's been packed in salt so it lasts for months and months. It's soaked in water or milk for 24 hours to remove the salt and can then be battered and fried.

The salt removes a lot of the natural water from the fish, so the batter stays incredibly crisp. The reason chip-shop batter goes soggy easily is because after a minute in newspaper all the natural water steams it. If you can't get salt cod, use normal cod fillets. I've tried seasoning them generously with salt half an hour before I cook them and once patted dry with a paper towel it really makes a difference.

Now, it's not particularly PC to promote cod fishing these days as supplies are being wrecked, so try to use a different white fish instead – hake or turbot – or the good organic farmed cod that's being produced at the moment.

A warning: when you're deep-fat frying, make sure small children are out of the way.

4 7–8-oz. white fish fillets, scaled and
  pinboned
sea salt
zest and juice of 1 lemon
3½ pints sunflower oil
2 egg yolks, preferably organic

1 scant cup flour, plus extra for dusting
olive oil
1 small (250ml) bottle of ice-cold fizzy
  mineral water
lemon halves, to serve

Season the fish really generously on both sides with salt and the lemon juice and put it on a plate in the fridge for at least half an hour, turning the fillets over a few times. Don't worry about them being too salty because a lot of the salt drains off with the moisture that comes out of the fish. After a while you'll notice that the cod has firmed up and there is a fair bit of moisture in the dish. Pour this off and pat the fillets dry with paper towels.

Pour your sunflower oil into a large, sturdy, thick-bottomed pan, making sure the oil reaches no more than two-thirds of the way up the side of the pan. Place the pan on a high heat, add a little piece of potato, and as the oil comes up to the right heat (325–350°F) you'll see it frying. While you're waiting for the oil to heat up you can make your batter. There's a traditional Italian batter on page 19 (the sage and anchovy fritters recipe), but I want to make this in a different, almost Japanese way. Put the egg yolks, flour, lemon zest, and a good glug of olive oil into a bowl and stir in the fizzy water until you get a custard consistency that will coat the back of the spoon. The bubbles in the water will make the batter lovely, light and crisp. Lightly dust each cod fillet with a little bit of flour and dip it into the batter, gently wiping it against the bowl so the batter doesn't get too thick. Carefully place your battered fish in the hot oil and fry for about 4 minutes, until golden and crisp. Feel free to fry the cod in smaller pieces to eat as nibbles. Really good. Serve with lemon halves.

la migliore frittata di gamberetti e prezzemolo

serves 2

the best shrimp and parsley frittata

To be honest, I'm a bit fussy about my frittatas. But this one hits the nail right on the head, especially when you get nice fresh shrimp, giving you an incredible sweetness that perfumes the eggs. When I made this, I was putting the lemon zest in with the eggs and, by mistake, I squeezed the juice of a quarter of a lemon in as well. I thought I'd try it anyway, even though you're not supposed to mix eggs with citrus juice. I think the result is spectacular – a lemon curdy shrimpy frittata ... but in a nice way!

The other key to this is to use plenty of parsley. Feel free to make smaller or bigger frittatas – most of the good ones I've eaten have ended up 1 inch thick. Any thinner and it's not a frittata. Any thicker and I think it gets frumpy. You can serve frittatas cold as an antipasto or hot as a snack, or even instead of a pasta course.

PS, This recipe also works brilliantly with crab or lobster.

6 large eggs, preferably organic
sea salt and freshly ground black pepper
a handful of fresh parsley leaves,
    finely chopped
zest of 1 lemon
juice of ¼ of a lemon

1 heaping tablespoon freshly grated
    Parmesan cheese
6–7 oz. fresh shelled medium shrimp
a good dollop of butter
olive oil
½ a dried red chili, crumbled

Preheat the oven to 425°F. In a bowl, whisk the eggs with a pinch of salt and pepper, then add the parsley, lemon zest and juice, and the Parmesan. Roughly chop half the shrimp, leaving the rest whole, and add all of them to the bowl. In a small, heavy, nonstick ovenproof pan, heat the butter with a good splash of oil until it begins to foam, then add all the egg mixture. Slowly move a spoon around the eggs for about a minute on a medium heat, then put the pan into the oven. (You often get frittatas that are very well cooked, but I'd rather have it in a hot oven for a shorter amount of time so there's a little color on top and the middle's cooked but not absolutely set.) Cook for 4 to 5 minutes, till slightly golden – it will rise slightly and will have a delicious lightness to it. Sprinkle the chili over it and slide it onto a board. Great served with a simple arugula salad, good bread, and a glass of wine.

Porchetta has to be one of the most quintessential Italian treats. It can be eaten on its own with a simple side dish like potatoes or vegetables, but is probably most often bought sandwiched between two pieces of *ciabatta*, with the occasional splodge of salsa verde, at a roadside stall or in the market. It's as prolific and normal there as fish and chips are to us in Britain. Even nowadays, lots of rural Italians, and some city dwellers too, still manage to keep pigs in their own back gardens – and I'm not talking about a couple of acres either, I'm talking small back gardens a couple of yards long – along with a few chickens and maybe some rabbits.

The relationship between most Italian people and pigs is an extremely proud one. Pigs are totally loved, respected, and celebrated in Italy, in a way that has sometimes been forgotten elsewhere. For Italians, prosciutto di Parma, made from the leg, is the Ferrari of cold meats and the charcuterie world; the loins and chops are roasted and grilled; the belly is prized for sausage and pancetta; the shoulder is rolled and turned into coppa di Parma, which is fantastic raw or cooked; not to mention lardo, a pure snowy white, dense, waxy fat which is cured like prosciutto and occasionally used in cooking but is more often eaten raw with a sprinkling of salt on top as part of an antipasti or charcuterie plate. The head is usually deboned, cured, seasoned with orange zest, and turned into coppa di testa, using the tongue, the cheeks, everything. But, in essence, not one part of the pig is disrespected or turned into a "dustbin" sausage. The nearest thing to a "dustbin" sausage I've ever seen in Italy (i.e. very finely puréed minced meat) is mortadella, and even this will have pistachios and truffles in it more often than not!

When buying your pork you're looking for the skin that is going to crackle the best – you want it not too wet and not too hard. To make life easy, ask your butcher for a half loin of pork from the rib end, with the skin and belly left on, and ask him to debone it for you. You will use the bones as a kind of trivet to cook the loin on, so make sure he gives you those too. Ask him to score right across the skin, about a half inch apart, through the skin and fat. This will save you half an hour of mucking about at home, and if you phone him in advance to ask him to do it I'm sure he'll be glad to help. Don't feel bad about asking, as this should be part of the

porchetta

the famous italian roast pork

serves 8

1 7–9 lb. loin of pork, on the bone
4 tablespoons fennel seeds
3 small dried chilies, crumbled
3 tablespoons rock salt, crushed
4 or 5 bay leaves, torn
1 lemon, zested and halved
olive oil
sea salt and freshly ground black pepper

2 sticks of celery, washed and roughly
 chopped
2 carrots, washed and roughly chopped
1 onion, peeled and roughly chopped
1 bulb of garlic, broken into cloves, unpeeled
12 sprigs of fresh rosemary
2 wineglasses of white wine
2 cups chicken or vegetable stock

Bone and score your loin of pork and place it skin side down on a cutting board. Preheat your oven to its highest setting. Using a pestle and mortar, a coffee grinder, or a metal bowl with a rolling pin, smash up the fennel seeds with the chilies and rock salt until you have a fine powder, then add the torn bay leaves and smash those up too. Mix in the lemon zest. Sprinkle the mixture evenly all over the pork meat, covering it completely.

Roll the belly around the loin and tie it tightly with 5 or 6 pieces of string to keep it all in place. Scatter the bones over the bottom of a snug-fitting appropriately sized roasting pan and put the loin of pork on top. Drizzle a little olive oil over the skin and season with salt, rubbing it into the scores. Place in the preheated oven, close the door, and immediately turn the oven down to 350°F. This way you will start the crackling off really hot and fast and the skin will puff up. The reduced temperature will then cook the meat through nice and evenly, keeping it moist at the same time. It will need to roast for about 2½ hours – feel free to leave it for a bit longer if you like. It just means the pork will be a bit drier but it will still be tasty.

When the meat has been cooking for an hour, add the roughly chopped celery, carrots, and onion to the pan with the broken-up bulb of garlic, the whole rosemary sprigs, and the wine. Give the pan a shake to get some fat onto the veg. When the pork is cooked, remove it from the pan and allow it to rest for 20 minutes. You'll have some nice roasted root veg and sticky goodness left in the bottom of the pan from which you can make your gravy. Pour off the fat and add a little of your stock, then give the gravy a stir, making sure you get all the lovely sticky brown bits off the bottom of the pan – you may not need to use all the stock. The Italians tend to keep their gravy light and more natural if using any, so this is the consistency you're after. Carve into thin slices with a sharp knife to serve.

PIZZA
Insaccati e Prosciutti
Mozzarella fresca
di latte intero o bufalo
Parmigiano Reggiano
Farine di prima scelta
Verdure di Stagione
Olio Extra Vergine di oliva
acqua , sale, lievito
Usiamo solo gli ingredienti migliori
MAMMA CHE PIZZA!
Sausages and Parma Ham
Fresh mozzarella cheese
(whole milk or buffalo)
Original Parmesan Cheese
First choice flours
Season's choice vegetables
Top choice Olive Oil
Water, salt, yeast
Flour
ciao

my thoughts on pizza

Pizza is probably one of the most famous dishes in the whole world. I was recently on a sourcing trip with my students in Tuscany and a terrific Neapolitan chef cooked for us. He told me that the first pizza ever in the world was the pizza fritta, and I've given you a recipe for it on page 59. It's basically a fried pizza which becomes incredibly light and is topped with cheese, tomato, and oregano before being grilled – delicious, absolutely delicious. It really knocked my socks off, but it also made me think of the simplicity with which pizzas should be considered. For instance, everyone is tempted to put too much on a pizza, and before you know it you have some version of a vegetable pie.

Very often tomato is the basis of a pizza topping, and mozzarella cheese is almost essential. When you eat good pizzas around Italy the toppings are normally very sparse and the base is rolled thinly. Just the sheer heat of the oven and the floor that the pizza is being cooked on gets the yeast into action to give you some lovely light bubbles. This year I went to a pizzeria in Naples that invented the Margarita pizza, and there was a big plaque on the wall to commemorate this achievement. To be honest, the pizzas at this restaurant weren't all that brilliant, and the service was diabolical, but the fact that Italians celebrate such simple dishes and argue about them and love them is what makes Italy one of the greatest food cultures in the world. In Italy I was informed that the way to eat pizza is to fold it in half and eat it like a man ... apparently anyone who uses a knife and fork is a jerk!

If you've got a half-decent large oven, you should try having a pizza party. Get your mates to bring the booze, and your job is to make a good base tomato sauce (see page 59), then go to a shop and buy some olives, basil, anchovies, and whatever other toppings you like and put them all out in dishes. Let your mates be responsible for creating their own toppings. You'll have such a laugh – I've always really enjoyed the pizza parties I've been to or held.

Apart from simple toppings, a thin good pizza base is important, and wood ovens do give them an amazing flavor and texture. However, not many people are going to have a wood oven at their house, so I've been on a quest to find the best way for you to cook a pizza that's even remotely authentic at home. The best thing you can do is to measure your oven and go and order a slab of marble or granite, about 1 inch thick, from a stonemason or a builder's merchant – you'll use this for years and years. You can preheat it in your oven at the highest temperature and it will absorb the heat almost like the base of a wood oven. Lay it on the metal bars, and when you're ready to start cooking, pull it out halfway and lay your pizza on top. It can also go straight onto the floor of an Aga stove's oven if you have one of those. It really will give you fantastic results. If you do fancy getting yourself a wood oven, I bought mine online as a kit. Even the small ones are good value – try doing your Sunday roasts in them – it gets you out in the garden!

pasta per pizza

basic pizza dough

This is a really simple method for pizza dough. If you can find semolina flour, it gives the dough an authentic flavor and texture.

1¾ lb. strong white bread flour
1½ cups fine ground semolina flour or
  strong white bread flour
1 level tablespoon fine sea salt

¼ oz. envelope active dried yeast
1 tablespoon golden caster sugar
just over 2 cups lukewarm water

Pile the flours and salt onto a clean surface and make a 7-inch well in the center. Add your yeast and sugar to the lukewarm water, mix up with a fork and leave for a few minutes, then pour into the well. Using a fork and a circular movement, slowly bring in the flour from the inner edge of the well and mix into the water. It will look like stodgy porridge – continue to mix, bringing in all the flour. When the dough comes together and becomes too hard to mix with your fork, flour your hands and begin to pat it into a ball. Knead the dough by rolling it backward and forward, using your left hand to stretch the dough toward you and your right hand to push the dough away from you at the same time. Repeat this for 10 minutes, until you have a smooth, springy, soft dough.

Flour the top of your dough, cover it with plastic wrap, and let it rest for at least 15 minutes at room temperature. This will make it easier to roll it thinly. Now divide the dough into as many balls as you want to make pizzas, i.e. lots of small ones or a few larger ones, but I suggest that 6 is a good quantity for this amount of dough.

Timing-wise it's nice to roll the pizzas out 15 to 30 minutes before you start to cook them. If you want to work more in advance, it's better to keep the dough wrapped in plastic wrap in the fridge rather than having rolled-out pizzas hanging around for a few hours. Take a piece of the dough, dust your surface and the dough with a little flour or semolina, and roll it out into a rough circle about ¼ inch thick. Tear off an appropriately sized piece of aluminum foil, rub it with olive oil, dust it well with flour or semolina, and place the pizza base on top. Continue doing the same with the other pieces and then, if you dust them with a little flour, you can pile them up into a stack, cover them with plastic wrap, and put them in the fridge.

When you're ready to cook them, preheat your oven to 500°F. At this stage you can apply your toppings. Remember: less is more. If you can, cook the pizzas on a piece of granite or marble in your conventional oven – if not, do them one by one on the bars of the oven shelf toward the bottom of the oven. (If you're going to cook your pizzas on the bars of the oven, make sure they're not too big – otherwise they'll be difficult to maneuver.) Cook for 7 to 10 minutes, until the pizzas are golden and crispy.

pizza toppings

Here are my eight favorite pizza toppings—the ingredients for each are enough for one pizza.

spicy salami, zucchini, basil, tomato, and mozzarella

4 tablespoons tomato sauce (see page 59)
6 thin slices of firm zucchini
8 fresh basil leaves
10 thin slices of spicy salami

3 oz. mozzarella
olive oil
sea salt and freshly ground black pepper

Smear your tomato sauce evenly over the pizza base. Lay on your zucchini and basil, then your salami – you want this to go on last so it goes crispy. Place small torn-up pieces of mozzarella into the gaps, drizzle with olive oil, and season with salt and pepper. Cook until crisp and golden (see page 54).

slow-roasted shredded pork with thyme, taleggio, and lemon-dressed arugula

When it comes to the meat, 2¼ lbs. of pork shoulder should give you enough pork to top about ten pizzas. Although the rest of the ingredients are for one topping, there is no point in cooking less pork than this – you can use any leftovers in sandwiches. This is also a great way to use up leftovers from a roast pork joint.

for the pork
2¼ lbs. pork shoulder
2 tablespoons fennel seeds
sea salt and freshly ground black pepper
olive oil

for each pizza topping
2 tablespoons tomato sauce (see page 59)
3 oz. taleggio cheese
1 teaspoon fresh thyme leaves
a small handful of arugula
juice of ½ a lemon

Preheat your oven to 325°F. Score the pork shoulder. Bash the fennel seeds in a pestle and mortar and rub them over the pork, then season and rub with olive oil. Roast in the preheated oven for at least 4 hours, until the meat is tender and shreds easily. When cool, shred up using a fork or your hands. Dress the meat with a little of the cooking juices – it will have almost the texture of a confit of duck.

Smear the tomato sauce thinly over the pizza base and scatter a small handful of your roasted pork and some small torn-up pieces of taleggio over it. Sprinkle with the thyme leaves, drizzle with olive oil, and cook until crisp and golden. Dress the arugula with a tiny bit of lemon juice, scatter it over the pizza and serve (see page 54).

potatoes, mozzarella, rosemary, thyme, and tomatoes

6 tablespoons tomato sauce (see page 59)
4 cooked new potatoes
a small handful of fresh rosemary leaves
1 teaspoon thyme leaves

extra virgin olive oil
lemon juice
sea salt and freshly ground black pepper
3 oz. mozzarella

Smear the tomato sauce evenly over the pizza base. Slice the potatoes into ¼-inch-thick slices and toss in a bowl with the rosemary, thyme, a good glug of olive oil, a small squeeze of lemon juice, and a pinch of salt and pepper. Scatter them over the pizza base and put small torn-up pieces of mozzarella into the gaps. Cook until crisp and golden (see page 54).

green and red grapes, rosemary, pinenuts, and ricotta

This might sound odd but it's totally delicious for breakfast or dessert. Especially with a ball of vanilla ice cream – great!

a handful of good red and green grapes,
  halved
1 tablespoon pinenuts
a small handful of fresh rosemary,
  leaves picked

2 tablespoons vanilla sugar
1 tablespoon white wine
1 heaping tablespoon crumbly ricotta
extra virgin olive oil

In a bowl mix together the grapes, pinenuts, rosemary, sugar, and white wine and allow to sit for a few minutes. Then scatter, with the juice, all over the pizza base. Crumble over little pieces of ricotta and drizzle with a little extra virgin olive oil. Cook until crisp and golden (see page 54).

egg, prosciutto, artichokes, olives, mozzarella, tomato sauce, and basil

6 tablespoons tomato sauce (see page 59)
2 baby artichokes (use good jarred ones)
3 slices of prosciutto
a small handful of good olives, pits
  removed

1 egg, preferably organic
3 oz. mozzarella
extra virgin olive oil
sea salt and freshly ground black pepper

Smear the tomato sauce evenly over the pizza base. Tear the artichokes into quarters and scatter over the pizza. Lay over the prosciutto slices and sprinkle the olives over them. Crack over the egg and place little torn-up pieces of mozzarella in the gaps. Drizzle with extra virgin olive oil and season with pepper and a tiny bit of salt. Cook until crisp and golden (see page 55).

smoked pancetta, mozzarella, fresh chili, and tomatoes

6 tablespoons tomato sauce (see page 59)
3 oz. mozzarella
1 fresh red chili, finely sliced

sea salt and freshly ground black pepper
5 slices of smoked pancetta, thinly sliced
extra virgin olive oil

Smear the tomato sauce evenly over the pizza base. Tear the mozzarella into pieces and dob these over, then scatter over as much chili as you like and season with salt and pepper. Lay the pancetta over the top so it will crisp up during cooking and the juices will cook into the pizza. Drizzle with extra virgin olive oil and cook until crisp and golden (see page 55).

mozzarella, anchovies, chili, capers, and parsley

Make sure you get hold of good-quality canned Spanish anchovies for this, otherwise it's not worth making it.

4 anchovy fillets
½ a fresh red chili, sliced
1 heaping teaspoon small capers,
  rinsed if salty
extra virgin olive oil
zest and juice of ½ a lemon

3 tablespoons tomato sauce (see page 59)
3 oz. mozzarella
1 tablespoon finely sliced fresh flat-leaf
  parsley
sea salt and freshly ground black pepper

Cut the anchovy fillets in half lengthwise and add to a bowl with the sliced chili – feel free to use as much as you like – the capers, a couple of tablespoons of extra virgin olive oil, and the lemon zest. Squeeze a little lemon juice on as well and mix up. Let the anchovies sit in the marinade for 15 minutes. Smear the tomato sauce evenly over the pizza base and scatter torn-up pieces of mozzarella over the top. Evenly lay on the anchovy fillets, scatter over the capers and chili, and sprinkle with a little parsley and seasoning. Drizzle with the leftover marinating oil and cook until crisp and golden (see page 55).

the best garlic bread

1–2 cloves of garlic, peeled
extra virgin olive oil

1 tablespoon sliced fresh flat-leaf parsley
sea salt and freshly ground black pepper

Smash the garlic up to a paste in a pestle and mortar and drizzle in 2 or 3 tablespoons of extra virgin olive oil. Smear this over the pizza base and sprinkle over the parsley. Season generously with black pepper and a little salt. Just before cooking, make little slashes along the pizza and pull it out to make small gaps as shown in the picture. Cook until golden and crisp, and drizzle with extra virgin olive oil just before serving (see page 55).

pizza fritta

fried pizza

When I took my students to Italy to see how olive oil was made, we ate these "fried" pizzas at a great little restaurant called Il Vescovino in Panzano in the Chianti region. The chef fried the thin bases in oil, like *poppadoms,* then quickly topped them with tomato sauce, mozzarella, and a little bit of oregano and popped them straight under a hot grill. They were the lightest pizzas I've ever eaten – just incredible – and this is how the first ever pizzas were made.

1 basic pizza dough (see page 52)
flour, for dusting
vegetable oil, for frying
2 5-oz. balls of buffalo mozzarella
optional: 5 teaspoons dried oregano

for the tomato sauce
extra virgin olive oil
1 clove of garlic, peeled and finely sliced
a bunch of fresh basil, leaves picked
1 14-oz. can of good-quality plum tomatoes
sea salt and freshly ground black pepper

First, make your basic pizza dough. While it's resting, make your tomato sauce. Heat a saucepan, add a splash of oil and the sliced garlic and cook gently. When the garlic has turned light golden, add half the basil, the tomatoes, and a few pinches of salt and pepper. Cook gently for about 20 minutes, mashing the tomatoes until smooth, then taste, season again, and put to one side.

Preheat your grill or broiler to its highest temperature. Divide the dough into 10 pieces and press them flat onto a floured work surface. Roll them out to about ¼ inch thick and allow them to rest for 10 minutes or so. Heat a frying pan over a high heat, add about ¾ inch of vegetable oil and fry each pizza for 30 seconds or so on each side. Remove with tongs and place on a baking tray.

Once all the bases are fried, smear each one with a spoonful of the tomato sauce and tear over some mozzarella and a leaf or two of basil or dried oregano. Drizzle with olive oil and grill until the cheese is bubbling and the dough is light brown and cooked through.

primi
first courses

UN AVE GIORNI 70 D'INDULIGENZA
1534.
MARIANO LAVENIA

soups

Soups from around the world have never really surprised me, however brilliant they are. In Japan I expected them to be brothy, clean, and fresh; in France I expected smooth, silky, elegant soups finished with cream, or made from a velouté (a roux made from fried flour and butter, with stock added a little at a time) and flavored with a whole army of fiddly garnishes. Then there are some predictable British soups, equally respectable but generally made from simple veg, native to Britain with French-style flutters.

But let's talk about Italian soups! When traveling around the country it was actually the soups that held the most surprises for me. They're rough and crude and full of personality – very much like some of the old Italian faces. They've got great depth of flavor and obviously have the benefit of the sunny Mediterranean climate and the vegetables and herbs that grow so readily there. Through hundreds of years of poverty, aspirational working-class families wanting to do better than just boiled water and bread have developed the soups we see in Italy today. A simple bread and water base would still be used, but as things like vegetables became more available, absolute show-stoppers like ribollita, a thick and delicious bread soup, and pappa al pomodoro, made with bread and tomatoes, came about. When the soil and the seasons dictated what produce was available, soups like minestrone (I like to think of it as "a harvest festival in a pot") would come into their own, tasting just delicious. Even if overcooked or made with leftover smashed-up pasta, minestrone can still be incredible.

The Italians, more than the natives of any other country I've been to, are accustomed to people just turning up and adding to the numbers at dinner, and the poor old mamas have got used to bulking out soups easily by adding pasta, bread, or beans – it's never seen as a hassle.

One thing I will say here is that you've probably heard me rave about good-quality extra virgin olive oil. And when I say that, I mean a $15 to $25 bottle of oil that tastes of a freshly mown lawn and has a little pepper to keep you on your toes. This quality of oil is always used to finish these soups off – it's by no means a basic commodity but is seen as a key ingredient. You don't have to use loads of it, so go and spoil yourself by buying a bottle – I guarantee you'll notice the difference. Anyway, now I'll stop raving and fantasizing and will just get on and make a bloody good soup – just don't expect steaming broths or Heinz tomato soup consistency like some of my restaurant customers do sometimes . . . we're in Italy now.

my thoughts on minestrone

Even though there are as many recipes for minestrone as there are villages in Italy, there are some golden rules that you need to remember in order to impress the most hard-to-please Italian.

• rule number 1 – the broth. **Minestrones can be made with water or vegetable stock, but the most memorable ones I've eaten have been made from the light broth that you get when making bollito misto (mixed boiled meats). I would suggest you either use a light chicken stock or do what I sometimes do – boil up a knuckle or hock of ham with a few pieces of smoked pancetta, some wine, peppercorns, and bay leaves and simmer it for a few hours. I then use the stock to make my minestrone. (The ham is fantastic served with beans or broken up on crostini.) Boiling ham like this sounds like a very British thing to do, but it's also widely done in Tuscany. So even though chicken stock will be fine, I thought I'd let you in on this secret so you can knock people's socks off.**

• rule number 2 – *soffritto.* **This means slowly, slowly frying vegetables (things like onions, celery, garlic, and, for this soup, carrots and fennel as well) to give you an amazing flavor base. It's an important first step when making a soup because it brings together and intensifies all the flavors. You'll see soffritto used in risotto bases, stocks, stews, and sauces across the whole of Italy.**

• rule number 3 – seasonality of ingredients. **Get the first two rules right, but if you serve this up to an Italian and the ingredients in the soup aren't seasonal and available at the local market, they'll think you're an idiot! So if it's winter and you're using asparagus and peas, that's wrong. If it's early summer and you're using Savoy cabbage (when you should be using asparagus and peas), that's not very clever either. So get your seasonal veg right. When I made this recipe, I was in Tuscany in early autumn. So it was a bit of a halfway house in terms of what veg were in season. There were no peas or fava beans left, but the cavolo nero and other cabbages hadn't yet had a good frost, so I decided to use Swiss chard, fennel, and zucchini – very nice.**

Follow these three rules and you'll find that you can take my recipe for early autumn minestrone on page 66 and make it your own. And don't forget – you know all those half-used bags of pasta at the back of your cupboard, with smashed-up bits at the bottom? Well, this is the perfect recipe for using them all up. Spaghetti is the pasta that is most often used in this soup, but using bashed-up bits is much more authentic, I think. It's also worth saying that dried and soaked, or canned precooked, beans work well, but if you can get hold of fresh ones from your local farmers' market, even better. Dried beans will need soaking overnight. (See page 256 for a recipe for cooking dried and fresh beans.)

minestrone d'inizio autunno

serves 4–6

early autumn minestrone

7 oz. cannellini or borlotti beans, fresh, or
  dried and soaked overnight
1 bay leaf
1 tomato, squashed
1 small potato, peeled
sea salt and freshly ground black pepper
olive oil
4 slices smoked pancetta or bacon,
  chopped
2 small red onions, peeled and finely
  chopped
2 carrots, peeled and chopped
2 sticks of celery, trimmed and chopped

½ a head of fennel, chopped
3 cloves of garlic, peeled and finely chopped
a small bunch of fresh basil, leaves and
  stems separated
2 14-oz. cans of good-quality plum tomatoes
2 small zucchini, quartered and sliced
a glass of red wine
½ lb. Swiss chard or spinach, washed and
  roughly sliced (including stalks)
2 cups chicken, ham, or vegetable stock
2 oz. dried pasta
extra virgin olive oil
a block of Parmesan cheese, to serve

Add your fresh or dried and soaked beans to a pan of water with the bay leaf, squashed tomato, and potato – this will help to flavor the beans and soften their skins. Cook until tender – check by tasting. They must be soft. Dried beans can take up to an hour, but check fresh ones after 25 minutes. Drain (reserving about half a glass of the cooking water), and discard the bay leaf, tomato, and potato. Now season with salt, pepper, and a splash of oil.

While the beans are cooking, make your soffrito. Heat a good splash of olive oil in a saucepan and add the chopped pancetta or bacon, onions, carrots, celery, fennel, garlic, and the finely sliced basil stems. Sweat very slowly on a low heat, with the lid just ajar, for around 15 to 20 minutes until soft, but not brown. Add the tomatoes, zucchini, and red wine and simmer gently for 15 minutes.

Now add the chard or spinach, stock, and beans. Put the dried pasta into a plastic bag, squeeze all the air out, and tie the end up. Bash gently with a rolling pin to break the pasta into pieces. Snip the end off the bag and empty the contents into the soup. Stir and continue to simmer until the pasta is cooked.

If you think the soup is looking too thick, add a little more stock or some of the reserved cooking water to thin it down a bit. Then taste and season with salt and pepper. Serve sprinkled with the torn-up basil leaves and with some extra virgin olive oil drizzled over the top. Put a block of Parmesan and a grater on the table for everyone to help themselves. Heaven!

pappa al pomodoro

serves 4

bread and tomato soup

This Tuscan soup is delicious – it's a soup everyone should try. Just thinking of it makes me salivate! It's a family-friendly soup – babies and grandparents (both without teeth!) can eat it with gusto. I've added roasted cherry tomatoes to my recipe but it also works really well just with canned tomatoes. The great thing is that it takes only 20 minutes to cook, so go for it! PS, Use a stale white country-style loaf – not cheap sliced white factory bread.

about 1 lb. ripe cherry tomatoes
3 cloves of garlic, peeled and finely sliced
a large bunch of fresh basil, leaves
  picked, stems finely chopped
the best extra virgin olive oil you can find

sea salt and freshly ground black pepper
2 14-oz. cans of good-quality plum tomatoes
about 1 lb. or 2 large handfuls of stale good-
  quality bread

Prick the cherry tomatoes and toss them with one sliced clove of garlic and a quarter of the basil leaves. Drizzle with extra virgin olive oil, sprinkle with salt and pepper, put them in a roasting pan, and cook in the oven at 350°F for about 20 minutes. The reason for doing this is so that their flavor becomes intense and concentrated.

Heat a glug of olive oil in a large pot and add the remaining garlic and the basil stems. Stir around and gently fry for a minute, until softened. Add your canned tomatoes, then fill the can with water and add that. Break the tomatoes up with a spoon, bring to a boil, and simmer for 15 minutes.

Tear the bread up into thumb-sized pieces and add them to the pan. Mix well and season to taste. Tear in the basil leaves and let the soup sit on a low heat for 10 minutes. By this time your roasted tomatoes will be done, with juice bursting out of their skins, so remove them from the pan, remembering to scrape all the lovely sticky bits from the bottom. Pour them into the soup with all the juices, basil, and oil from the pan.

Give the soup a good stir – you're looking to achieve a thick, silky, porridgy texture, so feel free to adjust it with a little water. Then remove it from the heat and add 6 or 7 tablespoons of extra virgin olive oil. Divide between your bowls and serve with a little extra basil torn over the top if you like. The most important thing with this soup is that you have a wonderfully intense sweet tomato basil flavor.

my thoughts on ribollita

Ribollita literally means "reboiled." Nowadays it is a Tuscan soup of beans, bread, and cabbage in its own right, but it was traditionally made using leftovers from soup made the day before. Any leftovers from that would become really thick, and could be fried in a pan with a little pork fat and turned into a kind of potato cake or patty – tremendous!

There's often confusion as to what ribollita should actually be like. It's not like minestrone, as it isn't brothy and it has no pasta in it. It's actually more like pappa al pomodoro, as it's thick and based on bread. It's very much Italian "peasant food" and would have been eaten a lot in the days of no central heating and lots of hard manual labor. I think this recipe embraces the heart and soul of what peasant cooking is all about – cheap, tasty power food. Please do make it and reheat it the next day – you'll find the flavors intensify.

Every year I take my students to Tuscany to see olive oil being pressed. On one trip, we were looking around three different estates in one day. Obviously we're thankful for any hospitality we're shown, and never want to seem impolite, but on this particular day we were served *four* ribollitas! It was certainly an education – no two were alike in the way they looked or tasted – they ranged from delicious to highly average, and from looking pretty and appetizing to looking like gray sludge. However, the ugliest ribollita was by far the tastiest, and unfortunately the prettiest one tasted like burned milk. A young lad had come in to make the ribollita for us that day – he let the bread catch on the bottom of the pan, but we ate it and carried on smiling!

Cavolo nero is the famous Italian dark cabbage, similar to kale – if you can't get it at your supermarket, you should be able to buy it at your local farmers' market. However, in its place you could use the outside leaves of a dark cabbage, like a Savoy or a dark kale, for instance. If you're a real foodie, order some cavolo nero seeds and sow them in your garden, like my dad and I do. We usually buy our seeds from a great place called Johnsons Seeds in Suffolk. Their website address is www.johnsons-seeds.com. (The kale seeds we order are called "Black Tuscany.") You can order cavolo nero seeds at www.localharvest.org. The beauty with cavolo is that you can grow it for six months of the year, and if you pick the outside leaves off as you need them, they'll just keep coming back – even in window boxes. Fantastic!

My favorite ribollita recipe is on page 72. In it I've suggested using zolfini beans. They are Tuscan white beans that are slightly smaller than cannellini beans, and they are incredibly creamy and delicious. Farmers are desperately trying to grow more of them in Italy, but the crops they get are quite low. Set your local specialty shop a challenge and ask them to try to get hold of some for you. Otherwise, use dried and soaked, or canned, precooked cannellini beans instead, as they work well in this soup. Don't forget that dried beans will need to be soaked overnight. (See page 256 for cooking dried and fresh beans.)

la mia ribollita preferita

serves 4–6

my favorite ribollita

11 oz. zolfini or cannellini beans, fresh, or
  dried and soaked overnight
1 bay leaf
1 tomato, squashed
1 small potato, peeled
2 small red onions, peeled
2 carrots, peeled
3 sticks of celery, trimmed
3 cloves of garlic, peeled
olive oil

a pinch of ground fennel seeds
a pinch of dried red chili
1 14-oz. can of good-quality plum tomatoes
11 oz. cavolo nero cabbage or kale leaves and
  stalks, finely sliced
2 large handfuls of good-quality stale bread,
  torn into chunks
sea salt and freshly ground black pepper
the best extra virgin olive oil you can find

Add your fresh or dried and soaked beans to a pan of water with the bay leaf, tomato, and potato – this will help to flavor the beans and soften their skins. Cook until tender – taste one to check that they're nice and soft. Dried beans can take up to an hour, but check fresh ones after 25 minutes. Drain (reserving about half a glass of the cooking water), and discard the bay leaf, tomato, and potato.

Finely chop your onions, carrots, celery, and garlic. Heat a saucepan with a splash of olive oil and add the vegetables to the pan with the ground fennel seeds and chili. Sweat very slowly on a low heat with the lid just ajar for around 15 to 20 minutes, until soft, but not brown. Add the tomatoes and bring to a gentle simmer for a few minutes.

Add the cooked and drained beans with a little of the water they were cooked in, and bring back to the boil. Stir in the sliced cabbage (it will look like loads, but don't worry as it will cook down), then moisten the bread with a little of the cooking water and stir it in too. The soup should be thick but not dry, so add a little more cooking water if you need to loosen it. Continue cooking for about 30 minutes – you want to achieve a silky, thick soup.

Season the ribollita with salt and pepper and stir in 4 good glugs of good-quality Tuscan extra virgin olive oil before serving, to give it a glossy velvety texture. Serve on a cold winter's day with lots and lots of Chianti!

zuppa di baccalà

serves 6

salt cod soup

Did you know that cod used to be a very highly prized, valuable trading commodity? Wars and battles were won on salt cod because, of course, in the old days ships were sailing for weeks or months and the sailors would have a very unhealthy diet. Having salt cod on board as a source of protein kept them going, and it meant they could jump off the boat with enough energy for a bit of fighting when it was required! All kinds of cultures began to salt fish – I suppose Iberian and Nordic countries are particularly well known for still doing it today. And certainly the Italians are more than partial to their fair share of it. Hundreds of years ago the only way to get fish into the center of Italy would have been to use preserved fish like salt cod. It might sound obvious, but this is why Tuscan cooking is predominantly meat- and bean-based. In the old days the only common fish recipes would have used either preserved or fresh lake fish.

Unless you live in a country where it's prevalent, like Portugal or Spain, salt cod can be bought only in good specialty markets. Try to hunt out the real *baccalà*, but if you can't find any then simply buy some fresh fish which can be salted overnight. As salt cod is preserved using copious amounts of salt, avoid seasoning this soup at all, or do it right at the very end.

11 oz. salt cod or 1½ lbs. fresh cod,
 haddock, or monkfish fillets
1 white onion, peeled
2 small carrots, peeled
2 sticks of celery, trimmed, pale green
 inner leaves reserved
2 cloves of garlic, peeled
a small bunch of fresh flat-leaf parsley,
 stems and leaves separated

extra virgin olive oil
1 small dried red chili, crumbled
2 14-oz. cans of good-quality plum tomatoes
1¾ cups light chicken stock
sea salt and freshly ground black pepper
juice of 1 lemon

If using fresh cod, haddock, or monkfish, pack it in a few handfuls of sea salt, refrigerate overnight, and rinse it before using. If using proper salt cod, soak the fillets in cold water for 24 hours, changing the water a few times during this period. This way, the fish will rehydrate and the saltiness will be removed before cooking. (If the fish is more than 1 inch thick it might need up to 36 hours' soaking.)

Chop the onion, carrots, celery, garlic, and parsley stems. Heat a splash of olive oil in a saucepan, and add the chopped vegetables, parsley stems, and dried chili. Sweat very slowly with the lid ajar for 15–20 minutes, until soft, but not brown. Add the tomatoes and simmer for 10 minutes, then add the stock and bring to a boil.

Break up any larger pieces of tomato with a wooden spoon and drop the salt cod fillets into the hot soup. Simmer gently for 15 minutes, just until the fish has poached and flakes apart when prodded with a fork. Pick out any bits of skin. Gently fold the flakes of fish through the soup, taste, and season with pepper, salt (if needed), and a little lemon juice. Chop the parsley and celery leaves and scatter over the soup. Drizzle with plenty of extra virgin olive oil.

pasta e ceci

pasta with chickpeas

It can be argued that this is both a soup and a pasta dish but I think it leans slightly more toward being a soup – so I've put it in this chapter! Its cousin, pasta e fagioli, is a thicker, redder bean soup, but I think that this simple, delicious dish, which uses chickpeas as its base, is what Italian food is all about . . .

1 small onion, peeled and finely chopped
1 stick of celery, trimmed and finely
  chopped
1 clove of garlic, peeled and finely
  chopped
extra virgin olive oil
a sprig of fresh rosemary, leaves picked
  and finely chopped

2 14-oz. cans of chickpeas
2¼ cups chicken stock
3½ oz. ditalini or other small Italian "soup"
  pasta
sea salt and freshly ground black pepper
optional: a small handful of fresh basil or
  parsley, leaves picked and torn

Put the finely chopped onion, celery, and garlic into a saucepan with a little extra virgin olive oil and the rosemary and cook as gently as possible, with the lid on, for about 15–20 minutes, until all the vegetables are soft, without any color.

Drain your chickpeas well and rinse them in cold water, then add them to the pan and cover with the stock. Cook gently for half an hour then, using a slotted spoon, remove half the chickpeas and put them to one side in a bowl.

Purée the soup in the pan using a handheld immersion blender. If you don't have one, you can whiz it up in a food processor instead, then pour it back into the pan. Add the reserved whole chickpeas and the pasta, season the soup with salt and pepper, and simmer gently until the chickpeas are tender and the pasta is cooked.

At this point, if the soup is a little thick, pour in some boiling water from the kettle to thin it down, and add more salt and pepper if needed. Serve drizzled with good-quality extra virgin olive oil. Lovely sprinkled with some freshly torn basil or parsley. A real treat.

il miglior brodo siciliano di aragosta   serves 4–6

the best Sicilian lobster broth

If you want to blow people's socks off, make this soup. I know lobsters are considered quite expensive, but for a special occasion it's worth pushing the boat out. Don't let the shops sell you precooked or dead lobsters – you need to get hold of live ones. Even the supermarkets should be able to offer live lobsters in this day and age, and if they can't, well . . . go and speak to the manager! You could also try making this soup using fresh shrimp, langoustines, or crab. The pici dough is incredibly simple to make, but feel free to use some smashed-up dried lasagne sheets or bashed-up spaghetti instead.

I'm confidently using cinnamon and almonds in this dish inspired by the Egadi Islands off the west coast of Sicily. They are near Tunisia, so their cooking has been influenced by all the Arabic and Greek invasions.

1 pici pasta dough (see page 105) or 6 oz. dried lasagne sheets, smashed up
2 2¼ lb. live lobsters
extra virgin olive oil
1 large white onion, peeled and finely chopped
6 cloves of garlic, peeled and finely chopped
1 large carrot, peeled and finely chopped

1 cinnamon stick
1 or 2 small dried red chilies, crumbled
1 teaspoon fennel seeds, smashed up
½ a bottle of white wine (Sicilian if possible)
3 cups tomato sauce or 3 14-oz. cans of good-quality plum tomatoes, blended
sea salt and freshly ground black pepper
a large handful of whole almonds, skins on
a small handful of fresh basil, leaves picked

Make your water pasta dough and roll it out into pici. If you're using dried pasta, get on with the soup right away. First of all, get a large pot onto a very gentle heat. Now, with live lobsters, the best and fairest thing to do is to get a large, sharp knife, place the tip on the little crown on the head and chop straight down between its eyes. If you want you can place a damp cloth or newspaper over the lobsters and put them in the fridge for half an hour beforehand. This makes them quite sleepy and relaxed. Once you've killed your lobster, twist and pull the head away from the tail. Do this to both lobsters and put the tails to one side with the claws. Open the lobster heads. Near the eyes there is a little gray stomach sac – I like to discard this. Then all you need to do is cut the head up into pieces, keeping all the brown meat and stuff.

Pour a couple of good glugs of olive oil into the hot pan and throw in all the head pieces and lobster legs. You can turn the heat up at this point. Throw in your onions, garlic, carrots, cinnamon stick, chilies, and fennel seeds. Continue moving and frying this soup base for around 15 minutes – you want to give the onions a little color, but don't let them burn. If the pan gets too hot, splash a little water into it.

Add your white wine and boil hard for 5 minutes before adding the tomato sauce and the same amount of water. Bring back to a boil, then reduce the heat and simmer for around 20 minutes to half an hour. Taste the broth – it should be becoming quite big and intense in flavor. At this point, put a colander on top of another large pot and carefully pass the soup through it. Press down on all the shells with the back of a ladle and let them drip for 5 minutes to really get all the flavor out of them. Once all the liquid has come out of the shells you can throw them away. Put the soup back on the heat to simmer – it should have a typical tomatoey soup texture. If it's thicker than this, let it down with a little water.

Slice the lobster tails across, through the shell and the meat, into 1-inch slices and put these into the broth. Crack open the claws, pick out the claw meat and add to the broth as well. Continue simmering for 8 minutes. Meanwhile, cook your pasta in salted boiling water, then drain and toss into the soup for 4 or 5 minutes.

Chop the almonds very finely or whiz up in a food processor and stir into the soup. Taste and season if needed. Divide between 4 bowls, tear the basil leaves over it, and drizzle with good extra virgin olive oil.

minestra di piselli di altamura

serves 4

altamura pea soup

When I was in Altamura in Puglia I worked with a family of bakers who all lived in the same big house. Each part of the family had its own living room and kitchen. I went back home with them one day and four different families were cooking four different meals – it was very surreal. This pea soup was one of the dishes being made. And it's so simple – just four ingredients and 15 minutes' simmering is all it takes. I've only ever made this soup with freshly shelled peas, but frozen peas work well too. If I'm using fresh peas, what I like to do to make the soup even more tasty is boil up the stock with the shells of the peas. You can do this while you're frying the onions. Then you can strain the stock onto your onions and peas when they're ready and fill the pan up again with water to boil your spaghetti while the soup simmers.

olive oil

2 medium onions, peeled and finely
  chopped

4 large handfuls of freshly shelled peas

2 pints chicken stock

9 oz. dried spaghetti, broken into approx.
  1-inch lengths

sea salt and freshly ground black pepper

optional: 1 sprig each of fresh mint, basil,
  and rosemary

extra virgin olive oil

a small handful of fresh flat-leaf
  parsley, chopped

Pour a good glug of olive oil into a pan, add the onions, and fry slowly for 10 minutes. Stir in the peas and chicken stock, bring to a boil, and simmer for another 10 minutes or so. Cook your spaghetti in salted boiling water for half the time it says on the package, then drain and add it to the pea soup to finish cooking. It's nice to tie up the sprigs of herbs and pop them into the soup to give it a nice fragrance, removing them before serving. When the pasta's cooked, have a taste of the soup and season carefully with salt and pepper. Divide the soup between the bowls, drizzle over a little extra virgin olive oil, and sprinkle with the parsley.

pasta

What on earth can I say about pasta . . . ? Well, if you want the real truth, the moment I stopped cooking sloppy, sticky, uninteresting, predictable pasta and started making pasta that was delicious, using the same commodities and ingredients that Italians use at home, was the moment my cooking changed forever. When my mentor, Gennaro Contaldo, told me a plate of pasta I'd cooked for him was the real deal and exactly how it would be done back home in Italy, it gave me loads of confidence and I was delighted.

Pasta is fun, and it should be made with love, then eaten quickly, with a lot of gusto and slurping if need be! But the best thing about it is the question I ask myself every time I make pasta from scratch . . . how fantastic is it that water, flour, and eggs – three everyday ingredients we all take for granted, and that are quite boring to look at – when mixed and kneaded together form an elastic dough that can be rolled, cut, or squashed into a million shapes, and flavored and colored a thousand different ways? It still amazes me! And then, with respect, intelligence, and utter simplicity, pasta can be combined with vegetables, fish, and meat – whatever the big man upstairs gives you – to make a delicious dinner that'll make you feel like you've had a big hug from an Italian mama!

Most of the recipes in this chapter use dried pasta, but I'm also going to give you two genius recipes for making it fresh – one using eggs on page 86 and one simply using flour and water in the pici con ragù recipe on page 105. Have a go at making them and enjoy it. Remember . . . it's just about the knack. It's not rocket science!

four generations of pasta-makers

basic recipe for fresh
egg pasta dough

makes enough pasta to serve 4

Try to get hold of Tipo "00" or another pasta flour – this is a very finely sieved flour which is normally used for making egg pasta or cakes. In Italy it's called farina di grano tenero, which means "tender" or "soft" flour. I normally use eggs to make my pasta, as here – you can either use 6 eggs or if you want to make it richer and more yellow use 12 yolks.

about 4 cups (1 lb. 6 oz.) Tipo "00" flour
6 eggs or 12 egg yolks, preferably organic

Place the flour on a board or in a bowl. Make a well in the center and crack the eggs into it. Using a fork, beat the eggs until smooth. Mix together with the flour as much as possible so it's not too sticky. Then flour each hand and begin to knead. This is the bit where you can let all your emotions out, so go for it! What you want to end up with is a nice piece of smooth, silky, elastic dough. Cover it with plastic wrap and leave it to rest for about half an hour in the fridge before rolling and shaping it.

pasta alla norma

serves 4

pasta norma style

This is a classic Sicilian pasta dish that everyone on the island grows up eating. (I haven't got a clue who Norma is, but I'm sure she's a good old girl!) I like this particular version because the eggplants are cut into strips rather than diced into cubes, and for some reason this seems to make them taste different. Also, adding oregano when frying the eggplants works so well. In Sicily the dish is finished off with salted ricotta – now, even though I can get hold of this easily in London, you might have some difficulty sourcing it, so feel free to use Parmesan or pecorino instead. PS, In the picture I crumbled some fresh ricotta over it instead of using the harder salted ricotta, as it works just as well.

2 large, firm eggplants
extra virgin olive oil
1 tablespoon dried oregano
optional: 1 dried red chili, crumbled
4 cloves of garlic, peeled and finely sliced
a large bunch of fresh basil, stems finely
  chopped, leaves reserved

1 teaspoon good herb or white wine vinegar
2 14-oz. cans of good-quality chopped plum
  tomatoes, or 2 cups passata
sea salt and freshly ground black pepper
1 lb. dried spaghetti
6 oz. salted ricotta, pecorino, or Parmesan
  cheese, grated

First of all, get your nice firm eggplants and cut them into quarters lengthwise. If they've got seedy, fluffy centers, remove them and chuck them away. Then cut the eggplants across the length, into finger-sized pieces. Get a large nonstick pan nice and hot and add a little oil. Fry the eggplants in two batches, adding a little extra oil if you need to (but you don't want to make it too greasy). Give the eggplants a toss so the oil coats every single piece and then sprinkle with some of the dried oregano – this will make them taste fantastic. Using a pair of tongs, turn the pieces of eggplant until golden on all sides. Once you've done the first batch, remove to a plate and do the same with the second batch.

When the eggplants are all cooked, add the first batch back to the pan – at this point I sometimes add a sneaky dried red chili, but that's my addiction coming through so feel free to ignore this! Turn the heat down to medium and add a little oil, the garlic, and the basil stems. Stir so everything gets evenly cooked, then add a swig of herb vinegar and the cans of tomatoes, which you can chop or whiz up, so they're not too chunky. Simmer for 10 to 15 minutes, then taste and correct the seasoning with salt and pepper. Tear up half the basil leaves, add to the sauce, and toss around.

Get your spaghetti into a pan of salted boiling water and cook according to the package instructions. When it's al dente, drain it in a colander, reserving a little of the cooking water, and put it back into the pan. Add the Norma sauce and a little of the reserved cooking water and toss together back on the heat. Taste the pasta and adjust the seasoning, then divide between your plates by twizzling the pasta into a ladle for each portion. Any sauce left in the pan can be spooned over the top. Sprinkle with the remaining basil leaves and the grated cheese and drizzle with olive oil.

linguine alla carbonara di salsiccia serves 4

sausage carbonara

This is like having a breakfast dish of pasta, and it is absolutely delicious! If you are a fan of sausages and eggs you'll love this combination. Not only does it look impressive, but it's so quick to make. There's a subtle line between having a smooth, silky egg sauce and scrambled eggs – both will taste delicious, but smooth and silky is far more desirable.

4 good-quality organic Italian sausages
olive oil
4 slices of thickly cut pancetta, chopped
sea salt and freshly ground black pepper
1 lb. dried linguine
4 large egg yolks, preferably organic

½ cup heavy cream
3½ oz. freshly grated Parmesan cheese
zest of 1 lemon
a sprig of fresh flat-leaf parsley, chopped
extra virgin olive oil

With a sharp knife, slit the sausage skins lengthwise and pop all the meat out. Using wet hands, roll little balls of sausage meat about the size of large marbles and place them to one side.

Heat a large frying pan and add a good splash of olive oil. Gently fry the sausage meatballs until golden brown all over, then add the pancetta and continue cooking for a couple of minutes, until it's golden. While this is cooking, bring a pot of salted water to a boil, add the linguine, and cook according to the package instructions.

In a large bowl, whip up the egg yolks, cream, half the Parmesan, the lemon zest, and the parsley. When the pasta is cooked, drain it in a colander, reserving a little of the cooking water, and immediately toss it quickly with the egg mixture back in the pasta pot. Add the hot sausage meatballs and toss everything together. The egg will cook delicately from the heat of the linguine, just enough for it to thicken and not scramble. The sauce should be smooth and silky. If the pasta becomes a little sticky add a few spoonfuls of the reserved cooking water to loosen it slightly. Sprinkle over the rest of the Parmesan, season if necessary, drizzle with extra virgin olive oil, and serve. Eat immediately!

linguine con cozze di nonno

grandad's mussel linguine

Nonno Contaldo is my mentor Gennaro's dad, but as far as Nonno is concerned, he thinks I'm his grandson. (You can make of that what you will!) When I went to the beautiful town of Minori on the Amalfi coast it was amazing to retrace Gennaro's youth – going up the mountains, down by the sea, meeting all his best mates. Everyone knew Gennaro and, of course, everyone knew Nonno. He's ninety-six years old, a little bit slow on his feet, but sharp as you like upstairs – just don't get him started on the war because he'll talk about it for hours. I was really impressed to find out that not only does Nonno live by himself, but he still cooks for himself every day too; although there are always friends and family nearby to help him if he needs it. His favorite dish to cook for himself is mussels with pasta, so I'm going to talk you through the recipe as he explained it to me.

Nonno gets his pot of salted water on to boil. If he has visitors he'll ask them to go down to the sea to get some water as this gives the dish a real authentic taste. He pours a few drizzles of extra virgin olive oil into a separate little pot and puts it on a medium heat. He adds a sliced clove of garlic, a tiny amount of crumbled dried chili (not too much), and an anchovy fillet. Then 6 ripe cherry tomatoes, halved, and squeezed into the pan as the garlic begins to fry. At this point Nonno adds 2 oz. of linguine to the boiling water, but I would suggest using about 3½ oz. At no point should the garlic take on any color, but you need the heat to be hot enough to melt the anchovies. The juice from the tomatoes and oil will make a light, very delicate and simple sauce. Now Nonno adds a good handful of washed and debearded mussels to the pan – he can taste the difference between bought mussels and wild ones, so he sent me down to the beach to pick some! They were slightly smaller, but he was right – the flavor that came out of them was worth so much more than having a bigger chunk of meat. He then gives the pot a little toss, places a lid on top, and cooks until all the mussels are open. (As usual with mussels, if any remain closed after cooking, throw them away.) He then adds a handful of chopped parsley to the pot.

The pasta will now be a little under al dente and only a minute away from being ready. Nonno likes to drain his pasta, saving a little of the cooking water; then he puts the pasta back into the big pot and pours the mussel sauce over the top, mixing everything together well. Then he puts the pot back on a low heat for an extra minute or two to cook the pasta perfectly – it will suck up all the lovely mussel juices. To finish, he drizzles over a good bit of extra virgin olive oil, seasons to taste, and serves immediately.

spaghetti con calamari

serves 4

spaghetti with squid

This is a fantastic Sicilian-style pasta dish which is really simple to make, but seems luxurious and posh at the same time!

olive oil
1 bulb of fennel, finely chopped and
  herby tops reserved
2 cloves of garlic, peeled and finely sliced
2 teaspoons fennel seeds, crushed
1 large glass of crisp Italian white wine
1 fresh red chili, deseeded and finely sliced
4 baby squid, cleaned and cut into rings,
  tentacles left whole

1 lb. dried spaghetti or linguine
sea salt and freshly ground black pepper
extra virgin olive oil
a small handful of fresh flat-leaf parsley,
  leaves chopped
zest of 1 lemon

Before you start, get all your ingredients prepped and ready to go.

Pour a couple of good glugs of olive oil into a large hot frying pan or casserole-type pan. Give it a swoosh around and add the chopped fennel, garlic, and fennel seeds. Fry on a medium heat for 5 minutes, stirring as often as you can. Turn the heat right up and add the wine, the chili, and the squid. Keep stirring until the alcohol and moisture have reduced by half. Turn the heat down to a slow simmer and now cook your pasta in salted boiling water according to the package instructions.

At this point taste the sauce and correct the seasoning. Once your pasta is nicely cooked to al dente, drain it in a colander, saving a little of the cooking water. Toss the pasta straight away with the squid and all the juices. Remove the pan from the heat and add about 5 tablespoons of really good extra virgin olive oil, along with the fennel tops and the parsley. Give everything a good toss, have one more taste to check for seasoning, add a little of the reserved cooking water to loosen if need be, then divide between 4 bowls. Sprinkle a little lemon zest over each plate and eat straight away.

rotolo di zucca e ricotta

rotolo of spinach, squash, and ricotta

Rotolo is a really unusual stuffed and rolled pasta dish. It takes a little longer than some other pastas, but it's worth the effort because it's such a joy to eat – a real showstopper if you want to turn heads. The one thing I would advise, though, is that you practice making it the week before your party. And make sure you have a very large pot or, even better, a fish kettle in which to cook it. (This is the dish that actually got me into writing books and doing all that sort of business, as it's what I was cooking in the background of a documentary when I was spotted all those years ago, so it's pretty close to my heart!)

1 lb. fresh egg pasta dough (see page 86)	2 cloves of garlic, peeled and finely sliced
½ a butternut squash, halved and deseeded	1¾ lb. spinach, washed
olive oil	½ lb. of unsalted butter
1 teaspoon coriander seeds	⅓ of a nutmeg, grated
1 teaspoon fennel seeds	5½ oz. crumbly ricotta cheese
½ a dried red chili	2 oz. freshly grated Parmesan cheese, plus extra for serving
sea salt and freshly ground black pepper	about 20 fresh sage leaves
a handful of fresh marjoram or oregano, leaves picked	

First make your egg pasta dough. Preheat the oven to 425°F. Chop the butternut squash into big chunks and rub them with a little olive oil. Bash up the coriander seeds, fennel seeds, and chili in a pestle and mortar with a good pinch of salt and pepper. Dust this mix over your pieces of squash, then put them into a snug-fitting ovenproof dish or roasting pan covered with a dampened piece of wax paper. Pop the pan into the oven for about 30 minutes, then remove the paper and let the squash roast for another 15–20 minutes, until golden. While this is cooking, get a large pan nice and hot and add a little olive oil, the marjoram or oregano, and the garlic. Move it all around for 20 seconds, then add the spinach. Water will cook out of it as it heats up – this is fine, though, as it will cook away. Using a pair of tongs, keep the spinach moving quickly around the pan, then after a minute add a couple of knobs of butter and the nutmeg and stir it around a bit more. Keep cooking until the moisture has cooked away, then season to taste and allow to cool.

To roll out your pasta either use a pasta machine to give you 4 or 5 long sheets (6 x 12 inches wide) and stick them together using a little water, or you can do what I do and use a rolling pin on a large surface, dusting with flour on top of and underneath the dough. Roll it out into a rectangular shape and trim it as necessary. Have a go at both ways. You want the dough to be the thickness of a beer mat and the size of a kitchen towel, then lay it out on top of a clean kitchen towel.

(continued on page 98)

Once you've done this, spoon a line of squash along the long edge of the sheet nearest you. Sprinkle the spinach over the rest of the sheet, leaving the top 2 inches of the pasta sheet clear. Crumble the ricotta over the spinach, sprinkle the Parmesan over it, and you're ready to begin rolling! Brush the last clear edge of the pasta sheet with a little water, then, working carefully, use the nearest edge of the towel to roll the pasta up and away from you, like a jelly roll. Roll the rotolo up in the towel and tie it firmly at each end using some string. You can secure the sausage shape even further by tying some more around the middle if you want. Tie a little extra string at one end so it can hang out of the cooking pot and act as a handle.

Now, to cook the rotolo, get your fish kettle or very large pot with a lid and fill it with boiling salted water. Lower the rotolo in and use the fish kettle rack on top to keep it submerged. If using a saucepan, hold the rotolo down with a plate. Simmer for about 25 minutes.

While it's cooking, you need to clarify some butter. To do this, take the remaining butter and place it in an ovenproof dish in the oven on a low plate-warming temperature (170°F). Over the next 10 to 15 minutes it will melt and you'll see that the milky whey will sink to the bottom. Discard any white bits floating on the top, then spoon out the clear golden butter and put to one side. Discard the whey. You won't need all the butter now, but it's quite hard to clarify any less than this – you can leave the extra in the fridge to use for your roast potatoes another day.

Now that you've removed the whey from the butter, you can heat it up more aggressively. So put about 3 tablespoons of your clarified butter into a pan and heat it up. Test to see if the butter is hot enough by adding a sage leaf to it. If it fries nicely, add the rest of the leaves and fry for about 30 seconds until they begin to crisp up. Then remove from the heat and put to one side.

When the rotolo is ready, carefully remove it from the pan, take the string off, unroll it, and slice it up – a couple of slices per portion. Scatter a few sage leaves over the top, drizzle with a little of your sage-flavored butter, and finish off with a sprinkling of grated Parmesan. Unbelievable!

the big pasta competition
in le marche

pasta con sarde

serves 4

pasta with sardines

This is a famous dish from Sicily, and one that all the kids there grow up eating. Sardines are one of the most economical fish in the market, literally a tenth of the price of something like shrimp. So this is real *cucina povera* (peasant cooking).

I've eaten this in so many restaurants – some of the tastiest looked quite gray and miserable because the sardines had cooked down so much. So I find the best thing to do is hold back some of the fillets and lay them on top of the dish for the last few minutes of cooking. This will give you a beautiful depth of flavor as well as lovely flakes of sardine. The finished dish has subtle sweetness from the onions and a nice heat from the chili which will really get your taste buds going. I've also eaten some lovely versions with chopped tomatoes added to them – you should definitely try this – but here's the basic one.

olive oil
1 large bulb of fennel, trimmed and
  finely chopped, herby tops reserved
2 small onions, finely chopped
1 heaping teaspoon fennel seeds, bashed up
2 or 3 small fresh red chilies,
  finely chopped
1 lb. 6 oz. sardines, scaled, gutted,
  and filleted

2½ oz./4 tablespoons pinenuts
1½ oz./2 tablespoons raisins
a wineglass of white wine
sea salt and freshly ground black pepper
extra virgin olive oil
1 lb. dried bucatini, spaghetti, or linguine
zest and juice of 1–2 lemons

Put 6 tablespoons of olive oil into a pan and place on the heat. Add the fennel, onions, fennel seeds, and chili and cook really gently, with a lid slightly ajar, for about 20 minutes without coloring the vegetables too much. You want to caramelize the fennel and onions so that the flavors are fantastic. Add half the sardines, the pinenuts, and the raisins and stir together well. Continue cooking slowly for a further 10 minutes with the lid off, stirring and mashing up every now and again, until the sardines have fallen apart giving you a rich base.

Add the white wine and a glass of water and cook until the liquid has reduced by half, then turn the heat down to a very slow simmer. Season to taste now, then lay the rest of the sardine fillets skin side up on top of the sauce, side by side, and drizzle with a little extra virgin olive oil. At this point put the lid on again and turn the heat to low so that the sardine fillets, which are thin anyway, will cook in the time it takes to cook the pasta – 7–10 minutes. Don't touch the sauce any more; don't mix it up, just let it continue cooking. Get your pasta on and cook according to the instructions on the package. When it's cooked al dente, drain and mix it into the sauce, drizzling in a little extra virgin olive oil, a good squeeze of lemon juice, and some of the finely chopped fresh fennel tops. Divide onto four plates, twizzling the pasta with your tongs as you do so, making sure you get some nice dense sauce on top. Sprinkle with some more fennel tops and some lemon zest, and serve immediately with a nice Sicilian white wine.

pici con ragù

serves 4

tuscan pici with tomato and meat sauce

This pasta, called pici, was made for me by Adriana, one of the housekeepers on the Petrolo estate. She showed me how to make it and made it look incredibly easy. When it comes to rolling out the pici, make sure you have a couple of thin wooden skewers handy and just press down very lightly using the ends of your fingertips.

1 lb. finely ground semolina flour, plus
  extra for dusting
approx. 1 cup water

for the ragù sauce
olive oil
1 red onion
2 cloves of garlic

3 bay leaves
a sprig of fresh rosemary
1 lb. 2 oz. ground beef or veal
4 14-oz. cans of good-quality plum tomatoes
sea salt and freshly ground black pepper
a block of Parmesan cheese, for grating

Place the flour in a bowl, and a little at a time, add just enough cold water to make a stiff dough. The drier the dough, the easier it will be when rolling it out later. Dust a clean work surface with flour and knead the pasta dough for 10 minutes or so until smooth and velvety. Wrap it in plastic wrap and refrigerate it until you are ready to use it.

Pull off an orange-sized piece of dough and roll it with your hands into a long, thin sausage shape on a very lightly flour-dusted work surface. When it's about 1 inch thick, cut it into 1¼-inch pieces so you end up with lots of little nuggets of dough.

Make sure the table or board is dry and free of flour, otherwise rolling will be difficult, and have a damp cloth nearby to moisten your hands. Take a 6-inch-long wooden skewer, hold it at both ends, and press it down lengthwise into a piece of dough as if trying to cut it in half down the middle. When you've pushed the skewer in halfway, roll the dough gently around the stick using your fingertips. You should end up with a very thin, sausage-shaped piece of pasta with the stick through the middle. When the pasta is rolled just thinner than a cigarette, stop rolling and gently pull it off, making sure you pull on the stick rather than the dough. Giving the stick a twist will also help. You should end up with a long, thin hollow noodle. Repeat with the rest of the dough and lay all your pici on a tray, dusted with semolina flour, to dry out slightly before using.

(continued on page 106)

When you have laid all the pieces out on a tray and dusted them with semolina flour, you can start to make the ragù sauce. Peel and finely chop the onion and garlic cloves, then heat a saucepan big enough to hold all the sauce ingredients. Add a splash of olive oil to the pan with the onion and garlic, and cook slowly for about 10 minutes, until soft and lightly colored. Add the bay leaves, the whole sprig of rosemary, the ground beef or veal, and the tomatoes. Stir well and bring to a boil. Turn the heat down and simmer gently for 2 hours with a lid on the pan. If the sauce starts to stick at any point, add a splash of hot water and stir well. Season well with salt and freshly ground black pepper. Using a pair of tongs, fish out the bay leaves and rosemary sprig and discard them.

Cook the pici in a pot of boiling salted water for around 10–15 minutes, until cooked through but still al dente. Drain and then stir them into the hot ragù sauce. Add a good splash of olive oil, then taste and season again if necessary. Serve with lots of freshly grated Parmesan.

fazzoletti di seta al pesto

serves 4

silk handkerchiefs with pesto sauce

Every village in Italy has its own way of shaping pasta. On the Ligurian coast they call these shapes "silk handkerchiefs" because they're light and delicate.

1 pesto recipe (see page 132)
1 lb. fresh egg pasta dough
  (see page 86)
flour, for dusting

3½ oz. freshly grated pecorino cheese, plus a
  little more for serving
a handful of fresh baby basil leaves

First make your pesto. Then make your egg pasta dough and roll it out to ⅛ inch or very thin on your pasta machine. Lay all the long strips on a well-floured worktop. Using a knife or a pasta wheel, cut the strips into rectangular pieces, roughly the size of coasters.

Cook the pasta in a large pot of boiling salted water for about 3 minutes, until just cooked, then drain, reserving a little of the cooking water. Toss the cooked pasta with the pesto and the pecorino. Taste and season if necessary, and add a few spoonfuls of the cooking water if you need to loosen the sauce up a bit. Serve sprinkled with more pecorino and the basil leaves, and tuck in straight away!

spaghetti tetrazzini

serves 4

chicken and mushroom pasta bake

I remember meeting a lovely old couple outside my parents' pub and when they heard I was going to Italy they told me to make sure I cooked turkey tetrazzini – I hadn't a clue what they were talking about and then, by chance, I saw a recipe for chicken tetrazzini in an old Italian cookbook and it's great – really tacky but gorgeous! Here's my version…

1 oz./a small handful of dried porcini
  mushrooms
olive oil
4 chicken thighs, boned, skinned, and cut
  into bite-sized pieces
sea salt and freshly ground black pepper
2 cloves of garlic, peeled and finely sliced

2 handfuls of mixed fresh mushrooms,
  cleaned and torn
1 cup white wine
1 lb. dried spaghetti
2¼ cups heavy cream
7 oz. Parmesan cheese, grated
a sprig of fresh basil, leaves picked
extra virgin olive oil

Preheat the oven to 400°F. Put your porcini mushrooms in a bowl and pour just enough boiling water over to cover them (approx. ⅔ cup). Put to one side to soak for a few minutes. Heat a saucepan big enough to hold all the ingredients, and pour in a splash of olive oil. Season the chicken pieces with salt and pepper and brown them gently in the oil. Strain the porcini, reserving the soaking water, and add them to the pan with the garlic and fresh mushrooms. Add the wine, with the strained porcini soaking water, and turn the heat down. Simmer gently until the chicken pieces are cooked through and the wine has reduced a little.

Meanwhile, cook the spaghetti in plenty of boiling salted water according to the package instructions and drain well. Add the cream to the pan of chicken, then bring to a boil and turn the heat off. Season well with salt and freshly ground black pepper. Add the drained spaghetti to the creamy chicken sauce and toss well. Add three-quarters of the Parmesan and all of the basil and stir well. Transfer to an ovenproof baking dish or nonstick pan, sprinkle with half the remaining cheese, and bake in the oven until golden brown, bubbling, and crisp. Divide between your plates, drizzle with extra virgin olive oil, and sprinkle with the rest of the cheese before serving.

pasta al forno con pomodori e mozzarella

baked pasta with tomatoes and mozzarella

This pasta dish is loved all over Italy. It is eaten by families at gatherings or celebrations and is also something the monks I visited at the Abbazia di Farfa, just outside Rome, have every Sunday as a special lunch. I'm pleased to say my faith in this dish has been restored, as I did fall out of love with it recently (as a result of trying to cook it in schools over the last year on a budget, using the cheapest pasta in the world). When I was in Altamura, in Puglia, I visited a school where they were eating baked pasta for their school lunch, bizarrely enough! However, Italian government laws state that the schools must use organic pasta and extra virgin olive oil, and they also had freshly made mozzarella! When made properly like this, it's absolutely delicious. This was the recipe that was made for one thousand kids at the school I visited and it was very, very good.

sea salt and freshly ground black pepper
extra virgin olive oil
1 white onion, peeled and finely chopped
2 cloves of garlic, peeled and finely sliced
1 or 2 dried red chilies, crumbled
3½ lb. ripe tomatoes or 3 14-oz. cans of good-quality plum tomatoes

a large handful of fresh basil leaves
optional: 1 tablespoon red wine vinegar
14 oz. dried orecchiette
4 big handfuls of freshly grated Parmesan cheese
3 5-oz. balls of mozzarella

Preheat your oven to 400°F and put a large pot of salted water on to boil. Heat a couple of glugs of extra virgin olive oil in an appropriately sized pan. Add your onion, garlic, and chili and slowly fry for about 10 minutes on a medium to low heat until softened but without any color. If you're using fresh tomatoes, remove the core with the tip of a small knife, plunge them into the boiling water for about 40 seconds until their skin starts to come away, then remove with a slotted spoon or sieve and remove the pan from the heat.

Put the tomatoes into a bowl and run cold water over them, then slide the skins off, squeeze out the seeds, and roughly chop. Add your fresh or canned tomatoes to the onion and garlic, with a small glass of water. Bring to a boil and simmer for around 20 minutes. Now put them through a food processor or blender to make a loose sauce. Tear your basil leaves into the sauce and correct the seasoning with salt, pepper, and a little swig of red wine vinegar.

When the sauce tastes perfect, bring the water back to a boil. Add the orecchiette to the water and cook according to the package instructions, then drain and toss with half of the tomato sauce and a handful of Parmesan. Get yourself an appropriately sized baking pan or earthenware dish and rub it with a little olive oil. Layer a little pasta in the pan, followed by some tomato sauce, a handful of grated Parmesan, and a sliced-up mozzarella ball, then repeat these layers until you've used all the ingredients, ending with a good layer of cheese on top. Pop the dish into the preheated oven for 15 minutes or until golden, crisp, and bubbling. Italians seem happy to eat this dish at room temperature or quite cold, but I prefer to eat mine hot.

spaghetti con gamberetti e rucola

serves 4

spaghetti with shrimp and arugula

This dish was on the menu in a little restaurant called La Gondola in one of the roughest parts of Palermo. I thought the combination of flavors was great, and very accessible to us back home in Britain. You can buy very high-quality frozen shrimp in supermarkets these days, so it's a win-win situation, but if you can get hold of some super-fresh ones and peel them yourself, this can all of a sudden become very luxurious in flavor. A real crowd-pleaser. Finish off with good-quality olive oil and wild arugula full of flavor and you'll be laughing. PS, If using frozen shrimp, make sure they're thawed out.

1 lb. dried spaghetti
sea salt and freshly ground black pepper
extra virgin olive oil
2 cloves of garlic, peeled and
  finely chopped
1–2 dried red chilies, crumbled
1 lb. peeled raw large shrimp

1 small wineglass of white wine
2 heaping tablespoons sun-dried tomato
  purée, or 6 sun-dried tomatoes blitzed
  in a blender
zest and juice of 1 lemon
2 handfuls of arugula, roughly chopped

Cook your spaghetti in a large pot of salted boiling water according to the package instructions. Meanwhile, heat 3 good glugs of extra virgin olive oil in a large frying pan and toss in the garlic and chili. As the garlic begins to color, add the shrimp and sauté them for a minute. Add the white wine and the tomato purée and simmer for a couple of minutes. When the pasta is ready, drain it in a colander, reserving a little of the cooking water. Toss the spaghetti with the sauce, squeeze in the lemon juice, and add half the chopped arugula, using a little of the reserved cooking water if you want to loosen the sauce a bit, and correct the seasoning. Divide between four plates and sprinkle with the grated lemon zest and the rest of the arugula leaves.

pasta con acciughe e pomodoro

serves 4

anchovies in tomato sauce with pasta

This is a poor people's pasta from Palermo in Sicily. You could use tagliatelle or spaghetti, but if you can find margherita pasta it's great – it looks thicker than spaghetti, and it's frilly down one edge. This sauce has great flavor and is very Sicilian with the raisins and pinenuts.

PS, I'd like to thank my mate John Hamilton, the incredible art director on this book, who made this dish with me in Sicily. He made it with such care and concentrated so hard staring at it that I thought it might turn to stone! As you can see from the picture it goes to show that even a Glaswegian geezer can produce a pretty and delicate dish.

olive oil
4 cloves of garlic, peeled and very
  finely sliced
2 big handfuls of pinenuts
a big handful of raisins
12 salted anchovy fillets

3 heaping tablespoons tomato purée
a large wineglass of red wine
1¾ cups stale breadcrumbs
1 lb. dried margherita pasta

Heat a pan, add 6 tablespoons of olive oil, then add your garlic and fry slowly. As it begins to color, add the pinenuts, raisins, and anchovies and continue frying for 2 minutes, until the anchovies have melted. Add the tomato purée and the wine and stir in well. Leave to simmer on a medium heat for 3 minutes. The sauce should be quite thick, like tomato sauce, but if you think it needs thinning down, add a little water. Heat a little olive oil in a separate pan, add the breadcrumbs, and fry until toasted, crunchy, and golden. Leave to cool on paper towels. Meanwhile, cook your pasta in boiling salted water according to the package instructions. Drain and mix with the sauce. Check the seasoning and divide onto 4 plates, twizzling the pasta with tongs as you go. Serve sprinkled with the breadcrumbs.

spaghetti alla trapanese

serves 4

spaghetti trapani style

OK, tigers – this could be your next favorite pasta! It's the Trapanese way of making a kind of pesto sauce, and it's so great with spaghetti. It's best made with ripe cherry tomatoes, but I ran out, so I've used normal ones in the picture. The sauce can be made in the time it takes to boil the water for your pasta and cook it. I prefer to make the pesto in a pestle and mortar, but I've used a food processor with good results too.

1 lb. dried spaghetti
sea salt and freshly ground black pepper
5½ oz. almonds, skins on or off
1 clove of garlic
4 large handfuls of fresh basil, leaves picked

5½ oz. freshly grated pecorino or Parmesan
  cheese
extra virgin olive oil
1½ lb. tomatoes, halved

Cook your spaghetti in salted boiling water according to the package instructions. Warm the almonds a little in a dry pan, then smash them up in a pestle and mortar or whiz them in a food processor until you have a coarse powder consistency. Put them into a bowl. Bash the garlic and basil separately in the mortar and mix with the almonds, adding the pecorino or Parmesan, a good glug of olive oil, and some salt and pepper. Add the tomatoes and really scrunch them with your hands into the almond mixture until they have completely broken up. Loosen with a little extra olive oil and toss with your hot drained pasta. Check the seasoning, divide onto 4 plates, and spoon any sauce that remains in the pan over the top.

making the grape-pickers' lunch,
petrolo estate, tuscany

lasagne alla cacciatora

hunter's lasagne

I made this for some grape-pickers at Petrolo. If you don't want to use five different meats you can just use one or two. See the arrosto misto recipe on page 224 – mix and match according to what's in season. You need 1 lb. 6 oz. of roasted, shredded meat for this recipe; here's a rough guide to how much picked meat you can expect from each animal: one hen pheasant gives 11–14 oz., one duck gives 14–18 oz., one pigeon gives 3½–5 oz., one wild rabbit gives 14–18 oz.; ask your butcher for a suitable weight and cut of venison.

1 lb. 6 oz. roasted, shredded meat
  (see above and page 224)
1 lb. fresh egg pasta dough
  (see page 86)
Parmesan cheese for grating
2 5-oz. balls of mozzarella
a handful of fresh sage leaves
olive oil

for the tomato sauce
olive oil
3 cloves of garlic, peeled and sliced
a sprig of fresh rosemary

3 bay leaves
3 14-oz. cans of good-quality plum tomatoes

for the white sauce
1¾ pints milk
a sprig of fresh parsley
a pinch of nutmeg
½ an onion, peeled and sliced
6 black peppercorns
6 tablespoons butter, plus extra for greasing
½ cup all-purpose flour
5½ oz. freshly grated Parmesan cheese
sea salt and freshly ground black pepper

Preheat your oven to 425°F, roast your meat, then make your egg pasta dough. When the meat is done, remove it from the oven. When cool, strip all the meat from the bones and place in a bowl with any crispy skin, discarding the rest of the skin and all the bones.

Heat a pan and add a splash of oil. Slowly fry the garlic until lightly colored, then add the rosemary, bay leaves, and tomatoes. Cook gently for 45 minutes with a lid on. When the tomatoes are nearly done, put the milk, parsley, nutmeg, onion, and black peppercorns into another pan and bring gently to a boil. Melt the butter in a third pan and add the flour. Mix well, then strain the milk and add it a ladleful at a time, stirring it in until you have a thick, smooth white sauce. Bring to a boil and simmer for a couple of minutes, then take off the heat, add the Parmesan, and season. Add your shredded meat to the tomato sauce, with a little hot water if it's too dry, and season. Simmer for 20 minutes, stirring every now and then. Remove the rosemary and bay.

Preheat the oven to 350°F and butter a large baking dish. Bring a pot of salted water to a boil with a good glug of oil and roll out your pasta into long strips about 3 x 10 inches. Blanch 2 or 3 strips at a time, then cover the bottom of the dish with pasta strips, letting them hang over the edges. Top with some meat sauce, then some white sauce and a sprinkling of Parmesan, and repeat the layers until you've run out of meat. Keep back enough white sauce for a final layer, then fold over the pasta from the edges and top with the white sauce. Sprinkle with Parmesan, tear over the mozzarella, scatter your sage over, and drizzle with olive oil. Bake in the preheated oven for 45 minutes or so, until golden.

the very full and content
grape-pickers after their lunch

risotto

You're going to absolutely love this chapter – as far as I'm concerned it includes some of the strongest risotto recipes I've ever done. I'll be totally honest – I didn't actually learn them from a mama or a nonna, although the method is the traditional mama style; I merely made them with the fantastic ingredients I came across in the markets. But that's surely what it's all about. They look great and they taste great and I'm really pleased with them all. Take the combination of chopped parsley in a white risotto with roasted mushrooms – it gives a different flavor to the basic risotto bianco. So, so good! (And if a local Italian turns his nose up, well, I don't care, because in this chapter I consider myself a know-it-all!)

I met a few young mothers on my travels around Italy, and what was interesting was that even though a lot of British people would consider a risotto an event in cooking terms, these young mums cook them because they're so damn simple and take only 20 minutes to make. Risotto is considered fast food, because while it's slowly simmering you only need to give it a quick stir every couple of minutes, meaning that you can get on with other small jobs at the same time. In other words, you don't have to be chained to the stove while it's cooking.

If you have lots of time, feel free to make your own chicken stock. However, since I became a dad three years ago I now either buy fresh stock in a tub from the supermarket or I use some organic veg bouillon and throw in a couple of dried porcini to give it some real ballsy flavor. I've seen loads of Italians do this as well, so I'm not going to feel like I'm not in the risotto club if I don't make fresh. And you shouldn't either!

If you're making risotto for a dinner party, it's not much more work to cook it for twenty people than it is for four – all you need to do is divide it into a couple of smaller pans and serve these in the middle of the table with a ladle in each one. Keeping it in the pans will also help to keep the risotto nice and moist.

risotto bianco

white risotto

This is a great basic recipe – it can be stretched in so many different ways to turn it into fantastically flavored risottos.

2 pints stock (chicken, fish, or vegetable, as appropriate)
2 tablespoons olive oil
a dollop of butter
1 large onion, peeled and finely chopped
2 cloves of garlic, peeled and finely chopped
½ a head of celery, trimmed and finely chopped

2 cups risotto (Arborio) rice
2 wineglasses of dry white vermouth (dry Martini or Noilly Prat) or dry white wine
sea salt and freshly ground black pepper
5 tablespoons butter
4 oz. freshly grated Parmesan cheese

Stage 1: Heat the stock. Put the olive oil and butter into a separate pan, add the onion, garlic, and celery, and cook very slowly for about 15 minutes without coloring. This is called a *soffrito*. When the vegetables have softened, add the rice and turn up the heat.

Stage 2: The rice will now begin to lightly fry, so keep stirring it. After a minute it will look slightly translucent. Add the vermouth or wine and keep stirring – it will smell fantastic. Any harsh alcohol flavors will evaporate and leave the rice with a tasty essence.

Stage 3: Once the vermouth or wine has cooked into the rice, add your first ladle of hot stock and a good pinch of salt. Turn the heat down to a simmer so the rice doesn't cook too quickly on the outside. Keep adding ladlefuls of stock, stirring and massaging the creamy starch out of the rice, allowing each ladleful to be absorbed before adding the next. This will take around 15 minutes. Taste the rice to check if it's cooked. If not, carry on adding stock until the rice is soft but with a slight bite. Don't forget to check the seasoning carefully. If you run out of stock before the rice is cooked, add some boiling water.

Stage 4: Remove from the heat and add the butter and Parmesan. Stir well. Place a lid on the pan and allow to sit for 2 minutes. This is the most important part of making the perfect risotto, as this is when it becomes amazingly creamy and oozy like it should be. Eat it as soon as possible, while it retains its beautiful texture.

risotto bianco con pesto

serves 6

white risotto with pesto

Once you've cracked the basic white risotto on page 130, it is great topped with a dollop of freshly made pesto – the combination of flavors is just fantastic.

a handful of pinenuts
½ a clove of garlic, peeled and chopped
sea salt and freshly ground black pepper
3 good handfuls of fresh basil, leaves picked and chopped

a good handful of freshly grated Parmesan cheese
extra virgin olive oil
1 risotto bianco (see page 130)

First make your pesto. Put your pinenuts on a baking sheet and pop them under the broiler for a minute or so – no more – just to warm through, not brown. This will enhance their flavor. Pound the garlic with a little pinch of salt and the basil leaves in a pestle and mortar, or pulse in a food processor. Add a bit more garlic if you like, but I usually stick to ½ a clove. Once pureéd, remove to a bowl, then bash the pinenuts to a mush and add to the basil. Add half the Parmesan, stir gently, and pour in some olive oil – you need just enough to bind and loosen the sauce to give an oozy consistency. Season to taste, then add most of the remaining cheese. Pour in some more oil and taste again. Keep adding a bit more cheese or oil until you are happy with the taste and consistency.

Make your risotto bianco. At the end of Stage 4, divide it between your plates and top with a dollop of your pesto. Really nice sprinkled with a few extra pinenuts, some freshly grated Parmesan, and a few basil leaves.

risotto ai frutti di mare

serves 6

seafood risotto

This risotto is something very special. You will need a mixture of seafood – try red mullet, monkfish, bream, John Dory, cod, mussels, clams, shrimp, and a little sliced squid. You can either use bought fish stock to make this risotto or you can have a go at making your own, as I do here. (Ask your fish store for the fish heads to use in the stock – these usually go into the trash, so you shouldn't be charged for them.) I'm going to make it in a slightly different way from the normal method, where I would fillet the fish before adding the bones and fish heads to the stock, so bear with me!

3 pints water
2 small carrots, roughly chopped
3 tomatoes, squashed
1 bay leaf
a small bunch of fresh parsley, one sprig
  left whole, remaining leaves picked and
  finely chopped
3½ lbs. mixed seafood (see above), scaled,
  cleaned, gutted, with heads and gills
  removed, mussels debearded

1 risotto bianco (see page 130)
½ a bulb of fennel, finely chopped, herby
  tops reserved
1 teaspoon fennel seeds
a pinch of crumbled dried chili
a pinch of saffron strands
extra virgin olive oil
juice of 1 lemon

Put the exact amount of water into a large pan with the carrots, tomatoes, bay leaf, and whole parsley sprig and bring to a boil, adding your whole fish but not your shellfish. Simmer for 10 minutes, then remove each fish from the pan and flake the flesh away from the bones. (If you have a cod head, try to remove the cheeks as they're the best bit!) Put the flaked fish on a plate to one side; return any bones to the stock to simmer for another 15 minutes max, skimming any froth off the surface every so often. Meanwhile, start your basic risotto bianco, adding the fennel, fennel seeds, chili, and saffron to the pan at Stage 1.

Pass the stock through a colander into another pan and throw away the vegetables and bones. Add most of the fish stock to your risotto, keeping a little to finish the dish. When the rice is nearly cooked toward the end of Stage 3, add your flaked fish and shellfish. After 3 or 4 minutes the shellfish will have opened (discard any that remain closed); then remove from the heat.

As you're not supposed to mix cheese and fish in pasta or risotto dishes we're not going to finish it with Parmesan. Instead, at Stage 4, when you add the butter, check the seasoning, drizzle with a glug of extra virgin olive oil, and squeeze over the lemon juice. To serve, divide the risotto between your plates and spoon over the remaining stock. Drizzle with some more extra virgin olive oil and sprinkle with the remaining parsley and the reserved fennel tops.

risotto ai carciofi

serves 6

artichoke risotto

Even though artichokes are a really everyday ingredient in Italy, in the UK and U.S. they do feel very luxurious. This is a basic risotto bianco with very thinly sliced artichokes added to it, which give it a wonderful perfume. You need small artichokes for this dish – not the large globe ones. When things like artichokes or zucchini are sliced thinly, the Italians call this *trifolati,* which literally translates as "in the style of truffles," i.e. wafer thin.

6 small or violet artichokes
zest and juice of 1 lemon
1 risotto bianco (see page 130)
sea salt and freshly ground black pepper

a small bunch of fresh mint, leaves picked
extra virgin olive oil
Parmesan cheese, for grating

Peel the artichokes back to their pale, light leaves, then halve them and remove the hairy chokes with a teaspoon. Immerse the artichokes in water with half the lemon juice, with a heavy lid or heat-resistant dish placed on top of them to keep them immersed and stop them from discoloring.

Start your risotto bianco and when you begin Stage 3 drop 6 of your prepared artichoke halves into the simmering stock. Continue cooking the risotto, adding the stock a ladleful at a time until the rice is half-cooked. Slice the remaining artichoke halves very finely and stir into the risotto. Continue stirring the stock into the rice. At Stage 4, when the rice is cooked and you add the butter and Parmesan, stir in the rest of the lemon juice. Take the pan off the heat and check the seasoning.

Remove the cooked artichoke halves from the stock pan and toss with most of the lemon zest, the torn-up mint leaves, and a splash of olive oil. Spoon the risotto onto 4 plates and place the dressed artichokes on top. Drizzle with any remaining dressing from the bowl and serve sprinkled with extra Parmesan and the rest of the lemon zest.

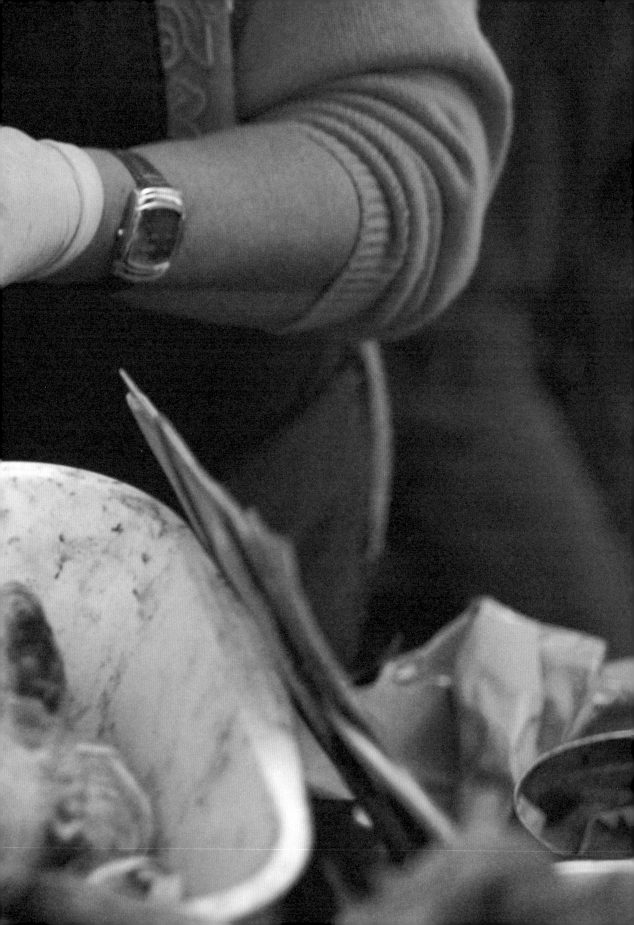

risotto ai cavolfiori

cauliflower risotto

serves 6

This is an absolutely delicious recipe. It's quite unusual, and the best thing about it is that it makes a hero of the much-underloved everyday cauliflower. If you're down at the farmers' market, or at the supermarket, have a look around for a Romanesco cauliflower – it's a similar size to a normal cauliflower but spiky and green. It also has a delicious flavor. The reason I love this dish is because it takes some all-time classic ingredients and puts them together in a great way. In Britain we normally eat cauliflower baked with cheese, and in Italy it is baked as a parmigiana with cream, cheese, and anchovies. All these flavors are in this risotto, with the added bonus of really crunchy chili *pangrattato* sprinkled on top – it gives an amazing kick.

2 handfuls of stale bread, torn into pieces	1 cauliflower
1 small can of anchovies, oil from can reserved	1 risotto bianco (see page 130)
	a handful of chopped fresh parsley
3 small dried red chilies	sea salt and freshly ground black pepper
extra virgin olive oil	Parmesan cheese, for grating

Whiz the bread in a food processor with the anchovies, the oil from the can, and the chilies. Heat a frying pan with a splash of oil and fry the flavored breadcrumbs, stirring and tossing constantly until golden brown.

Trim the coarse leaves off the cauliflower and cut out the stalk. Chop the nice inner part of the stalk finely. Start making your risotto bianco, adding the chopped cauliflower stalk to the pan with the onion and celery at Stage 1. Add the cauliflower florets to your pan of hot stock.

Continue to follow the basic risotto recipe, adding the stock bit by bit until the rice is half-cooked. By now the cauliflower florets should be quite soft, so you can start to add them to the risotto with the stock, crushing them into the rice as you go. Continue until the rice is cooked and all the cauliflower has been added.

At Stage 4, when you add the butter and Parmesan, stir in the parsley, taste, and season. Sprinkle with the anchovy *pangrattato*, grate some more Parmesan over the top, and serve. So, so good!

risotto ai funghi e prezzemolo

serves 6

roasted mushroom risotto with parsley

This is just a beautiful risotto recipe and a great one if you're a veggie. By roasting the mushrooms you get a real depth of flavor and this is set off brilliantly by the strong, clean flavor of the parsley. It's big and ballsy and you'll love it!

1 risotto bianco (see page 130)
7 oz. wild mushrooms, cleaned and torn
olive oil
sea salt and freshly ground black pepper
1 bulb of garlic, cloves peeled and halved
a small bunch of fresh thyme, leaves picked

1 tablespoon butter
a small bunch of fresh flat-leaf parsley, very finely chopped
1 lemon
Parmesan cheese, for grating

Preheat the oven to 400°F. Start making your risotto bianco. When you come toward the end of Stage 3, you need to roast your mushrooms, so heat a heavy-bottomed ovenproof frying pan or baking pan until medium hot and add a splash of oil. Fry the mushrooms for a minute or two, until they begin to color, and season with salt and pepper. Add the garlic, thyme, and butter and mix together. Place the pan in the preheated oven and roast the mushrooms for 6 minutes or so, until cooked through and rich in flavor.

At Stage 4 of your risotto recipe, when you add the butter and Parmesan, stir in all the parsley – this will give you a fantastic green color and perfumed flavor. Roughly chop half the roasted mushrooms and garlic and stir into the risotto, adding a good squeeze of lemon juice to balance the flavors. Divide between your plates and sprinkle over the remaining mushrooms. Serve with grated Parmesan.

risotto ai finocchi con ricotta e peperoncino

serves 6

fennel risotto with ricotta and dried chili

To me, fennel is a really tasty, classy, and underused vegetable. It works really well with the ricotta in this recipe and has a fantastic sweetness. Please don't buy the crappy ricotta that a lot of the supermarkets have – make sure it's light and crumbly and, if you're out of luck, a fresh goat's cheese is pretty damn good too.

½ teaspoon fennel seeds
extra virgin olive oil
2 cloves of garlic, peeled and finely sliced
2 bulbs of fennel, finely sliced, herby
  tops reserved
sea salt and freshly ground black pepper

1 risotto bianco (see page 130)
2 small dried chilies
4 tablespoons good crumbly ricotta
zest and juice of 1 lemon
Parmesan cheese, for grating

Put your fennel seeds into a pestle and mortar and bash up to a powder. Get a wide, hot saucepan, add a couple of splashes of olive oil, and fry the garlic until softened, then add the bashed fennel seeds and sliced fennel. Add a pinch of salt and pepper and turn down to a medium-low heat. Place a lid on the pan and cook nice and slowly for around 20 minutes, until the fennel's soft and sweet.

Start the risotto bianco as usual and continue through the recipe until the rice is half-cooked. Halfway through Stage 3, stir in the sautéd fennel, then keep cooking the risotto until the rice is perfectly cooked.

Bash up the dried chilies in the pestle and mortar until you have a fine powder. At Stage 4, when you add the butter and Parmesan, add the crumbled ricotta and lemon zest. Check the seasoning carefully and balance the flavor with as much lemon juice as you feel it needs to work with the fennel. Divide between your plates, sprinkle your fennel tops over the risotto, and dust with the ground chilli. Grate over some fresh Parmesan at the table.

one of the most exciting cooking
moments of my life – this shepherd
thought my risotto was "ottimo"

risotto con cipolle bianche dolci, cotechino, e timo

serves 6

risotto of sweet white onions, cotechino sausage, and thyme

Cotechino or zampone sausage is the big hero in this dish. You should be able to buy these, or order them at least, from any good Italian deli (and if they can't get them for you, then they're not a good Italian deli). They come already cooked in a vacuum-sealed bag. If you pop them out of the bag, they can be roasted happily with the onions for quite a long time, and have a wonderful flavor, but if you can't get hold of one I'd suggest simply cutting open a good-quality fresh Italian-style or coarse sausage and breaking it into the basic risotto at the beginning, when frying off your onions and celery. PS, This is also good with cooked cranberry beans stirred in at the end.

1 lb. cotechino sausage
3 white onions
1 risotto bianco (see page 130)
sea salt and freshly ground black pepper

a small handful of fresh thyme,
  leaves picked
Parmesan cheese, for grating
extra virgin olive oil

Preheat the oven to 375°F. Place the cotechino in a small roasting pan with the unpeeled onions and pop into the preheated oven. Bake for about an hour, until the onions are soft and sweet and the sausage is cooked. Remove everything from the oven and turn it down to 300°F.

Start the risotto as usual and continue through the recipe, adding the stock little by little. While doing this, you'll have plenty of time to peel the cooled onions. Cut one of them into quarters, put them in a dish, and keep them warm in the oven. Finely chop the other 2 onions, peel the thick fatty skin off the sausage, and discard it. Crumble up the sausage meat inside. When the rice is three-quarters cooked, at Stage 3, stir in the chopped baked onions and the crumbled sausage, and continue cooking the risotto until the rice is perfectly cooked.

At Stage 4, when you add the butter and Parmesan, taste, season carefully to perfection, and fold in the chopped thyme leaves. Divide between your plates, break up one of the onion quarters over each, and serve sprinkled with grated Parmesan and a drizzle of extra virgin olive oil.

insalate *salads*

salads

One of the things I've noticed in Italy is how the quality of their salads can vary from one place to the next. Half of the time you'll probably get given rubbishy unwashed iceberg lettuce, with a little tray of condiments so you can dress your own salad, and the other half of the time their salads can be pure genius – above and beyond those of any other country in the world. In general, this is down to their ability to turn boring old carrot, celery, fennel bulb, and pepper into a delicious salad just by cutting them into thin slices that are delicate and crunchy. The Italians are very clever people. Even unexpected things, like Jerusalem and globe artichokes, asparagus, baby zucchini, even butternut squash, are really palatable in a salad when finely sliced. But probably the most impressive thing is their use of stale bread – something you may not think of as a good salad ingredient!

This is the first year that I've grown lots of my own vegetables. If you want to have a go at doing this, salad leaves are a brilliant way to start. All you need to do is buy yourself an organic tomato grow-bag, cut it open, order some salad seeds from my mate Jekka McVicar, at www.jekkasherbfarm.com, or from www.seedsofchange.com or www.seedsavers.org, and even if you live in the middle of a city you can be cutting your own salad leaves four or five days a week for four months a year for hardly any money at all. The best thing about them is that the more you cut them the faster they grow – even an idiot like me can grow them successfully!

In Italy salads are eaten as a matter of course, very often after the secondo. If you've never been to Italy, some of the recipes in this chapter will reinvent what you perceive as a salad. And if you're not the salady type, you just don't know what you're missing. In comparison to Italy, it's horrific to see what the British consider a salad. No wonder lots of people here think they don't like them. If you are one of these people, I hope this chapter helps to change your view.

panzanella

tuscan bread, tomato, and pepper salad

Wow, now we're getting into the territory of real Italians. What I mean by this is the territory of arguing profusely and passionately, with very large hand movements, about the best way to serve a ribollita, or the best way to cook the perfect pizza, or the best version of this salad!

So what is a panzanella? Well, it's a traditional Tuscan bread salad devised to use up stale leftover bread. It started out as peasant food or farm workers' food, as it was cheap to make but also very filling. Nowadays you can find it as an *insalata* on a restaurant menu.

2 red bell peppers
2 yellow bell peppers
1 lb. 6 oz. good-quality stale bread
2 lb. 3 oz. ripe mixed tomatoes
sea salt
6 salted anchovies or 12 anchovy
  fillets, in olive oil
a handful of small capers, washed
1 red onion, peeled and halved

1 celery heart
a large handful of fresh basil, leaves picked

for the dressing
good-quality red wine vinegar
good-quality extra virgin olive oil
1 small clove of garlic, peeled
sea salt and freshly ground black pepper

Whether you've got an open fire (like I had where I was staying in Tuscany) or a gas burner or simply a broiler, get the heat going full whack. Place the peppers directly on the flame or under the broiler and allow them to blister and blacken for 10 minutes. Using tongs, turn them over so that each side gets done. When they're blackened all over, put them in a bowl and cover with plastic wrap. Allow them to steam in the bowl for 20 minutes – this will make it easy to remove the skins.

Now, when I say stale bread I mean good stale bread – at least a day old. Don't go and buy a loaf to use straight away. I generally tend to go for a country-style loaf, and obviously the better quality it is, the nicer the salad will taste. You can use a large *ciabatta* but please don't go using a loaf of white sliced. Remove any hard excess crust and rip the bread into thumb-sized pieces. The wonderful thing about tearing the bread into pieces is that, one, you don't need a knife, two, it will open up the pores of the bread to suck up the juices better, and, three, the bread will look like it's from a farmhouse and not a factory. Pop the pieces of bread on a pan and put them next to the oven to dry out while you get on with the other bits.

So your tomatoes should be at kept room temperature. Don't store them in the fridge like my wife does! Give them a quick wash and chop them into pieces similar in size to the bread. It's great to use different colors too. Evenly but lightly season the tomatoes with sea salt and put them in a colander with a bowl below it to catch the juice. Now, into this bowl where the juice is dripping, you're going to put your anchovy fillets and capers. Try to get good-quality salted whole anchovies and peel the fillets away from the bone with your fingers under the tap.

(continued on page 156)

If you can't find whole anchovies, Spanish fillets in oil are good, and you can add them straight to the bowl. I find that the sweetness of the tomato juice actually removes any excess salt from the anchovies. In turn, they give the juice a bit more flavor, which is what we want because we're going to turn that into the dressing.

The next job is to slice the red onion as finely as you can. Remember – a little piece of onion is a joy in a salad but a ruddy great chunk is about as classy as a dodgy old doner kebab! Then you need to do the same with the celery heart. Now, what is a celery heart? Well, it's the pale inner part of the celery, so click about five or six pieces of celery off and then remove the top 6 inches. These parts can be used in sauces or stews – but for this salad we're only interested in the heart, as it's not so stringy. Also, the beautiful yellow leaves can be sprinkled on top later, so put them aside. Finely slice the heart and put it into a large bowl with the onions, then add the bread.

If the peppers have cooled enough, remove as much black skin as possible, as well as the stalk and seeds. But don't be a cowboy chef and rinse them under the tap or you'll lose all the sweetness and flavor down the drain. Once you've done this, tear them up into slivers about the size of your little finger. Add them to the onions, celery heart, and bread.

Give the tomatoes a little toss in the colander and press them lightly to remove any excess liquid – you should have a fair bit of juice in the bowl below if they have been sitting for 20 minutes. At this point remove the anchovies from the bowl of juice and put them to one side. Add the tomatoes to the rest of the salad. Tear up most of the basil leaves and add them too.

What I normally start off doing with the tomato juice dressing is to add 2 tablespoons of good-quality red wine vinegar to the tomato juice and capers. If you haven't got any, a sherry vinegar or good white wine vinegar is OK. Then add about 10 tablespoons of good-quality extra virgin olive oil – good ones always come in dark bottles and cost around $12–$25. This may sound expensive, but it really is worth using the good stuff on this salad.

Grate or crush the garlic and add it to the dressing. Mix the dressing around and have a little taste. You want it to be a bit acidic and quite feisty because all the bread and peppers will knock the zing out when they soak it up, so if you go slightly over the top you'll probably find it comes in at 10 out of 10 once the flavors have had time to infuse. Add salt and pepper, if you think it's needed, then pour the dressing all over the salad ingredients in the large bowl. Without being too rough, give the salad a good toss for about a minute.

I think panzanella is best served in one large bowl in the middle of the table and then everyone can help themselves. So once you've mixed it, tasted it, corrected the seasoning, and tossed it again, clean up the edges of the bowl and then drape the anchovies evenly over the top of the salad. Flick over the celery leaves, a little extra basil, and an extra drizzle of olive oil. Leave the salad for 15 minutes before eating it – but it will sit happily on the table for up to an hour.

You may be thinking this recipe sounds like a bit of a fuss for a salad and, yeah, opening a bag of prewashed leaves is much quicker, but the number of times I've made it and then just roasted a chicken in a little oil, salt, and pepper and eaten them together on a nice summer's day . . . it's an absolute joy and is really worth it. So give it a go.

insalata tipica delle sagre

festival mixed salad

serves 6

This is a fantastic mixed salad and one that varies from place to place in Italy at the local food festivals (*sagras*) where ingredients are celebrated. The reason the salad can be so interesting and have so many different ingredients is that when it's made it's generally going to be large, so it's worth buying lots of different bits and pieces to give it crunch, color, sweetness, and loads of character. The Italians, more than most, love to use fresh veg – I've even seen some of them use finely shredded raw asparagus, which is really unusual. When you're shopping, just remember to have a look at different leaves, crunchy fennel, cucumber, radishes, but feel free to buy a little bit of everything. If you can't find all the ingredients I've listed, don't worry. It's about getting a mixture of different things, so feel free to substitute here and there.

When I was in Tuscany I made this salad for thirty-five grape-pickers – it took me about half an hour to prepare it, which I think is pretty good going. More than anything it just comes down to a little bit of assembly. If you need to make it for more than six people it's easy to bulk it out with other interesting things like yellow bell peppers, different kinds of cress, and fresh herbs like mint or basil.

1 red bell pepper, halved and deseeded
a small handful of fresh flat-leaf parsley
3 or 4 tomatoes
10 radishes
½ a cucumber, peeled, halved, and deseeded
½ a bulb of fennel
1 Belgian endive
½ a round lettuce, such as Boston
½ a frisée lettuce

½ an oakleaf lettuce
a handful of arugula
½ a radicchio

for the dressing
1 heaping tablespoon capers
4 good-quality anchovy fillets, in olive oil
3 tablespoons red wine vinegar
good-quality extra virgin olive oil

Finely slice the red pepper and put it into a bowl. Slice the parsley leaves and finely chop the stems. Cut up the tomatoes and finely slice the radishes, cucumber, fennel, and Belgian endive.

In the sink, wash your round lettuce, the central yellow part of the frisée (which is not bitter – discard the outer leaves), the oakleaf lettuce, and the arugula. Then spin the leaves dry and tear them up. Wash the radicchio, remove the core, and shred it. Add all these leaves to the bowl and mix them up well to give you a really colorful-looking salad.

To make the dressing, either chop up the capers and anchovies or whiz them in a food processor. Put them into a bowl and add the red wine vinegar and three times as much olive oil. Have a taste – it will be reasonably pungent. Feel free to adjust the vinegar and oil, but remember that you want the vinegar to cut through a little because by the time you've tossed it with the leaves it will mellow a lot. Don't worry about seasoning – you shouldn't need any because the capers and anchovies are salted. Mix the dressing well, pour over the salad, and toss together. Serve straight away.

insalata di radicchio e rughetta
radicchio and arugula salad

Radicchio, like other bitter leaves such as Belgian endive, dandelions, cicoria, and treviso, becomes extra special when its bitterness is balanced with other tastes – like the sweetness of balsamic vinegar, the saltiness of Parmesan, or the crunchy pepperiness of arugula. Sometimes in life you have one particular thing which, on its own, is nothing, yet mix it up in the right combination and somehow it becomes genius – it's like this with recipes, and especially this one.

Get yourself a large bowl and, for each person, toss together a handful of arugula with a small handful of grated Parmesan cheese and a quarter of a radicchio, finely sliced. Dress this with a glug of balsamic vinegar, three times as much extra virgin olive oil, and a little salt and freshly ground black pepper. Mix carefully, grate over a little extra Parmesan, and eat straight away. You can vary it by adding things like toasted pinenuts, roasted red onions, or crispy bacon.

insalata di gennaro

gennaro's salad

Essentially this is an Italian-style Niçoise salad. It's not particularly surprising that the Italians would have their own version of this, because great tuna and anchovies are two of their staple foods. This recipe doesn't have olives or French beans in it though, which are an essential part of the original French way. The main thing you need to remember is to dress the potatoes while they're still steaming hot, so they'll take in more of the lovely flavors. My mate Gennaro used to make this for our staff lunch when I worked with him and it's delicious!

14 oz. new or small waxy potatoes
4 large eggs, preferably organic
2 heaping tablespoons salted capers
2 lemons
1 6- or 7-oz. can of really good tuna in oil,
   drained, or 11 oz. fresh tuna
sea salt and freshly ground black pepper
for fresh tuna: a good pinch of
   dried oregano

for fresh tuna: ½ a fresh red chili, chopped
good-quality extra virgin olive oil
a large handful of arugula
a large handful of mixed salad leaves, torn
1 small red onion, peeled and finely sliced
4 salted anchovies, rinsed, boned,
   and filleted

Give the potatoes a little scrub. Bring a pan of water to a boil and add the potatoes to it, then season the water with salt. Put a lid on and boil fast until the potatoes are tender and you can put a knife through them. At the same time, boil your eggs for 7 or 8 minutes so that they are firm but soft-boiled. Refresh them in cold water, then shell them and put to one side.

While the potatoes and eggs are cooking, wash the capers under the tap, then drain them and pop them into a bowl with the juice of one of the lemons squeezed over to draw out any excess salt. If you're using fresh tuna, all you need to do is put it into a nonstick pan with a little olive oil, a sprinkle of oregano, salt and pepper, and a little chopped chili. Simply sear it so it remains pink in the middle, or, if you prefer, fry it for a few minutes on each side until cooked through – but don't overcook it. Wash the salad leaves and spin them dry.

By now your potatoes should be done. You need to dress them while they're still really hot, so drain them quickly in a colander, then halve or chop them into a bowl. Add the capers and lemon juice, 5 tablespoons of extra virgin olive oil, a pinch of salt and pepper, and the finely sliced onion and toss together really well. Taste a potato to make sure the seasoning is just right – you may want a little more oil or lemon juice. When they are getting down to room temp you can flake in the tuna, be it canned or freshly cooked, then add the salad leaves and the halved or quartered eggs. Drizzle a little extra virgin olive oil over, mix carefully, divide between four plates, and lay the anchovies over the top.

insalata amalfitana

amalfi salad

The citrus fruits grown on the Amalfi coast are the best in the world, so I've included oranges in this salad out of respect to them. (My lord, I can't believe I just wrote that – I must be getting old!) It is so easy to make, but it does help if your knife skills are remotely good because then it will be quick quick quick. If not, you can invest in one of those sharp slicers called a mandolin, but watch those fingers. Speed peelers are great to use for this salad too. All you need to do is keep peeling – it doesn't matter if the veg aren't uniform. The idea is that the thinner you can slice everything, the nicer the salad will be.

This is the kind of salad that is eaten at the start of an Italian feast or meal, as it cleans the palate and has wonderful flavors. Even though totally untraditional, it's also bloody marvelous with some crumbled feta cheese or a good goat's cheese over the top, as both of these work really well with orange.

1 bulb of fennel, washed
1 red onion, peeled
1 cucumber
a large handful of radishes, with tops, washed
optional: a small handful of ice cubes

2 tablespoons good-quality herb or red wine vinegar
good-quality extra virgin olive oil
sea salt and freshly ground black pepper
4 oranges, peeled, segmented, and seeds removed

Remove the herby tops from the fennel and put them to one side, then trim the fennel at both ends and, if need be, lose the outside layer – it's sometimes a bit dry. Split the fennel in half and slice lengthwise as finely as possible. Put into a large bowl. Remove both ends of the onion, then halve it and slice it as finely as possible. Slice the cucumber finely. When it comes to the radishes, leave about ½ inch of stem on them. Then slice a little off each radish, roll it onto the flat edge, and finely slice.

If you want to throw a few ice cubes in the bowl and toss them together with everything, bizarrely enough this does cause the veg to go even crunchier. Just keep them in there for a few minutes. The cowboy way of doing this is to add the veg to iced water, but if you've ever done that then, yes, the veg goes crunchy, but most of the flavor drains into the water.

Remove the ice cubes from the sliced vegetables. In a bowl mix together 2 tablespoons of good herb or red wine vinegar and 6 or so tablespoons of a good-quality extra virgin olive oil. Mix well, then taste. You might want to add a little extra vinegar, depending on how sweet your oranges are. Taste and season with salt and pepper. Dress the salad with this and then add the orange segments and any juice. Toss a few times, then divide between your plates and sprinkle with the saved fennel tops. Serve straight away.

insalata di pomodori, finocchi, e seppie

serves 4

tomato, fennel, and squid salad

This is a beautiful summery salad, using grilled squid with tomatoes and fennel. It's a fantastic combination, and it makes a great starter or lunch. Make sure you ask your fish store to do the gutting, skinning, and opening out of the squid for you. They may even open out the white bodies and gently score the squid in a crisscross pattern if you ask. This means the squid will cook really nicely. When it comes to tomatoes, there seem to be so many to choose from these days – buy what tastes good when you're shopping. I think it's always a nice idea to get a few different types of tomato to make the salad more interesting. The key to this salad is not to make it until just before you're ready to cook the squid.

4 medium squid, gutted, cleaned, and skinned, tentacles and wings kept separate	juice and zest of 1 lemon
	juice of 1 orange
	1 teaspoon dried oregano
½ lb. mixed cherry and plum tomatoes, sliced, halved, or quartered	good-quality red wine or herb vinegar
	extra virgin olive oil
½ a red onion, peeled and finely sliced	sea salt and freshly ground black pepper
1 bulb of fennel, plus herby tops	1 dried red chili, crumbled

Prepare your cleaned squid bodies by slicing them along one side and flattening them out if the fish store hasn't done it for you. Now score the inside flesh in a crisscross pattern with a knife. Slice, quarter, or cut the tomatoes into erratic chunks and put them into a bowl with the onion. Remove the herby tops from the fennel and put to one side. Cut the fennel in half, finely slice, and toss it with the tomatoes and onion. Squeeze in the lemon and orange juice and add the oregano. Dress the salad with 3 tablespoons of red wine or herb vinegar, 7 tablespoons of good-quality extra virgin olive oil, salt, and pepper, and toss around. Taste and correct the seasoning if need be.

The squid is best cooked over white-hot cinders on a barbecue, but you can also use a griddle pan or a large preheated frying pan. If barbecuing (see page 190 for my thoughts on barbecues), get the coals as close to the bars as possible. Season the squid with a little salt and pepper, sprinkle the dried chili over it, and pat with oil on both sides. Put the tentacles on first, as they take twice as long to cook as the body. When they've had a minute and a half, turn them over and add the white part of the squid (the body) crisscross side down. Don't turn the squid over until you see dark bar marks appear. You'll normally need to give it 3 to 4 minutes if using a hot grill, longer if not. Once colored on both sides, slice the squid up at an angle and throw the pieces, while still warm, into the bowl of tomatoes and fennel. Toss around, have one final taste to make sure you're laughing, and divide evenly between four plates. Drizzle with any extra juices and a little extra oil. Sprinkle with the lemon zest and herby fennel tops. Delicious served with lemon wedges on the side.

billy no-mates!

insalata caprese

salad from capri

serves 4

I was debating whether or not this recipe should go into the book, as there's probably a Caprese salad in every Italian cookbook around. However, they never seem to be done in the way that I like to make mine, because they're usually made with perfectly sliced mozzarella and tomato. So I wanted to do my take on this brilliant combination. The mozzarella is torn and the whole thing is more rustic, plus the dressing is made in a different way. It tastes absolutely delicious and has got to be one of the simplest salads you can do – it looks great served on a large platter. Just don't forget that this salad obviously originates from the island of Capri, where they have great weather and the tomatoes and basil are absolutely fantastic, so try to get hold of the best ingredients you can.

4 5-oz. balls of buffalo mozzarella
2 handfuls of good mixed ripe tomatoes,
  of different shapes and sizes
the white of 1 spring onion, very
  finely sliced
extra virgin olive oil
good-quality herb vinegar

for the dressing
a big handful of fresh basil leaves
sea salt and freshly ground black pepper
extra virgin olive oil

First make your dressing. Keeping a few leaves aside for later, roughly chop the basil and pound with a good pinch of salt in a pestle and mortar. Add a splash of oil and stir it in to make a lovely smashed basil dressing.

Carefully tear the mozzarella onto a large serving plate. Chop the tomatoes roughly into chunks and dress in a bowl with the spring onion, some olive oil, a little herb vinegar, and some salt and pepper. Place the tomatoes in and around the mozzarella and drizzle the basil sauce over the top. Sprinkle with the reserved basil leaves and serve.

insalata di farro con verdure al forno   serves 8

farro salad with roasted veg

Farro, also called spelt, is a grain similar to pearl barley, but it's dried in such a way that instead of being fluffy and spongy it becomes chewy and nutty. You may have difficulty getting hold of it, but if you can find it you'll be using it all the time – it has an unusual flavor halfway between rice and couscous (this recipe will also work well with both of these). In Italy it was a major food for the ancient Romans, who used it to make bread, porridge, and soup before they got hold of wheat. Nowadays it's used in salads, soups, stews, even pastas. You should be able to buy farro in good Italian markets, and supermarkets have started to stock it in the special selection aisles. Here's a recipe for one of my fave salads – give it a go.

14 oz. farro or bulgur wheat
3 yellow summer squash, halved
  lengthways and deseeded
2 zucchini, halved lengthways and
  deseeded
2 bulbs of fennel, trimmed and thickly
  sliced, herby tops reserved
1 red onion, peeled and cut into wedges
2 red bell peppers, halved, deseeded, and
  cut into chunks

2 eggplants, cut into chunks
4 cloves of garlic, peeled
extra virgin olive oil
sea salt and freshly ground black pepper
herb or white wine vinegar
a good bunch of fresh herbs (flat-leaf
  parsley, basil, mint, oregano)
a squeeze of lemon juice

Preheat the oven to 400°F. Soak the farro or bulgur wheat in cold water for 20 minutes, then drain. Slice the squash and zucchini across into chunky half moons and put them into a large roasting pan. Add the remaining vegetables and the garlic cloves and toss together with a good splash of olive oil. Season well with salt and pepper. Try to spread the vegetables out in one layer, as they'll roast better this way (use 2 pans if you have to). Roast in the preheated oven for 30–40 minutes, removing the pans and carefully shaking them now and then, until the vegetables are cooked through and crisp around the edges. Sprinkle a little vinegar over the vegetables as soon as they come out of the oven, and set aside to cool. When cool, tip onto a large cutting board, add the fresh herbs, and chop finely.

Place the farro or bulgur wheat in a large saucepan, cover with fresh cold water, and bring to a boil. Simmer for 20 minutes, or until tender, and drain well. Dress with olive oil and the lemon juice, season with salt and pepper, and toss with the roasted herby vegetables. Scatter the reserved fennel tops over it and serve.

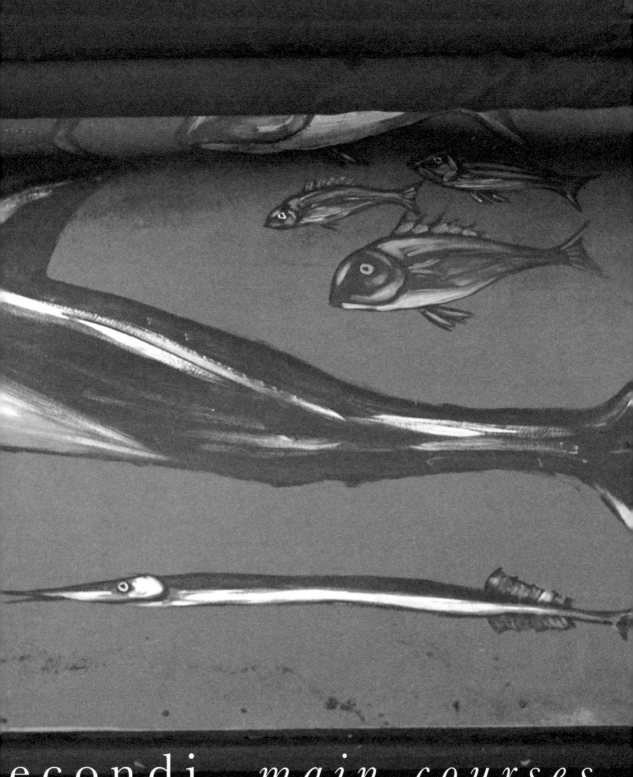

econdi *main courses*

fish

If I've learned anything from the Italians about fish, it is definitely that "less is more." Even inland, in regions like Le Marche and in Tuscany, they might get fish coming to the market only once a week, but it's still damn fresh and smells of the sea and is bound to make dinner a bit of an event on that day.

I was quite surprised at the number of seaside restaurants in Italy that don't have a menu, like La Scaletta, run by my friend Giovanni on the island of Marettimo. He literally waits till eight or nine in the morning, when the boats come in, and says, "Whatever God brings me, I will cook!" Of course, not having all the choice in the world does make you think cleverly about what you can do with what you've got. Even on a rough day when there's no catch, Giovanni will use preserved fish, which he keeps in his larder. Maybe half the problem these days is that we have too much choice and not enough quality. Which got me thinking that I wanted to keep the recipes in this chapter really simple. I've done this by adding some delicate twists to plainly cooked fish. There's nothing in this chapter that I don't think you could achieve, so give them all a go.

However, before you get down to cooking, there's one thing I'd like you to do for me . . . get to know your local fish store, be it a supermarket or an independent. If their fish smells "fishy" and not of the sea, then have a word and tell them you'd support them if they had less choice and better quality. I'm sorry to say there are too many halfwits selling second-rate fish in Britain and the U.S. these days. It shouldn't have to be like that. Take a city like London, for example. It's one of the biggest cities in the world, yet there are only a handful of fishmongers that come up to the mark. (In case you're wondering, my two favorites are Kensington Place and the Fishworks chain.) Young kids growing up all around our country think fish smells fishy, because that's the reality of the fish on offer to us in most places. So what I'd like to ask you to do is stop putting up with substandard products – be a bit more Italian and have your say on a regular basis. What fish stores and supermarkets alike will have to start doing then is worrying about quality, not quantity. If we all have a go, you'll be surprised how many shops, restaurants, and businesses will look at what they're doing because they have to listen to their customers. Let's make it happen!

rombo con finocchio

turbot with fennel

Whether it's a suckling pig or a fish, I think roasting something whole brings a lot of romance to a meal. It's also the best way to cook whole fish of any size and don't let anyone tell you differently! The bones give the meat incredible flavor and keep it moist while cooking.

In my world the turbot is the Aston Martin of all fish because it has the most juicy, white, meaty flesh. It also gets my Japanese friends going when they come to England! Turbot come in various sizes – the biggest I've ever seen was about 22 pounds. I've had fishermen ring me at the restaurant while still at sea to tell me they've just caught a big turbot and I've rewritten the menu to get it on that night, either baking it like this recipe, or in salt. Beautiful! You can also cook flounder or halibut the same way, or even big wings of skate, with similarly genius results. If you go for a bigger fish, you'll need to cook it for longer – test it with a small knife at the thickest part and if it comes away from the bone easily it's ready.

Don't worry if you can't get hold of any fennel branches – you've got the seeds in there anyway, but using both is just fantastic. If you haven't got fennel growing in your garden, buy some to plant now. It's incredibly good-looking, tasty, and very hardy, and comes back year after year. You can always use parsley or basil, or you can lay a finely sliced fennel bulb on the bottom of the pan instead. It's an excellent flavor to have with both pork and fish.

1 whole 4½–6½-lb. turbot or flounder (gills
  and roe removed by your fish store)
1 tablespoon fennel seeds
1 tablespoon rock salt

a small bundle of fennel branches
2 lemons, finely sliced
olive oil

Preheat your oven to 400°F. Wash the turbot well, inside and out, and pat dry with paper towel.

In a pestle and mortar, grind the fennel seeds and rock salt to a powder. Sprinkle all over the fish and inside the cavity. Spread the fennel branches out in a large baking pan (big enough to hold the whole fish) and place the turbot on top of the branches. Lay the lemon slices in a row (as in the picture) or all over the fish and drizzle generously with olive oil.

Bake in the preheated oven for 35 to 40 minutes, or until the meat starts to come away from the backbone of the fish. You will notice some incredibly milky juices will cook out of the fish – you can turn them into a light, natural sauce by adding a good glug of olive oil and a squeeze of lemon juice. Serve in the pan at the table and let everyone help themselves.

polpo semplice

tender octopus

Fishermen regularly catch octopus in the waters around Britain. They're incredibly cheap to buy, but many people don't quite know what to do with them, so first of all I'm going to show you how to cook octopus until it's tasty and tender, with its own broth, and then on the next page you can find three delicious recipes derived from it. If your fish store doesn't normally sell octopus, ask them to order it for you. They should be happy to do this if you give them a few days' notice.

olive oil
1 bulb of garlic, peeled and finely sliced
1 fresh red chili, deseeded and finely sliced
3 or 4 parsley stems, finely chopped

strips of rind from 1 lemon
1 3½-lb. octopus
sea salt and freshly ground black pepper

Get yourself a large pot with a lid and put it on the heat. Add about 7 tablespoons of olive oil to the pot, then add the garlic, chili, parsley stems, and lemon rind. Fry slowly for a minute or two, without browning the garlic, then add the whole octopus to the lovely flavored oil. Give the pot a shake, put a lid on it, and turn the heat down to a steady but slow simmer. Over the next 15 to 20 minutes the octopus, depending on its size, will become deliciously tender. Lots of liquid will cook out of it, giving you a flavorsome natural broth. To check on its tenderness, stick a fork into it and if it slides through you're laughing. If not, leave it to simmer for a little longer. So this is your basic tender octopus.

In Italy it's normal to slice the whole octopus up and eat it straight away, seasoned with salt and pepper and drizzled with olive oil – or you can dispose of the skin and suckers as well as the brown meat from inside the head, the beak (mouth), and the eye, before slicing. This is all easy to do and I prepare and cook octopus in this way every time, no matter what. Now turn over to see how to make it in three different ways.

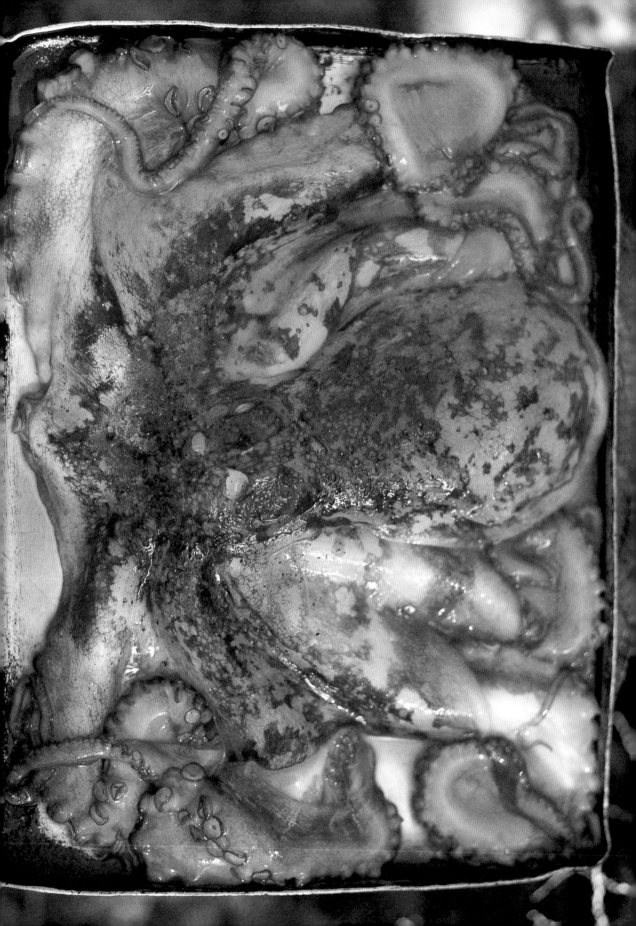

polpo in brodo *octopus in broth*

serves 6

1 tender octopus (see page 180)
a small handful of mussels, cleaned and
 debearded
a small handful of clams, cleaned
sea salt and freshly ground black pepper

3 or 4 sprigs of herby fennel tops, finely
 chopped
a small bunch of fresh flat-leaf parsley,
 leaves picked and finely chopped
extra virgin olive oil

When the octopus is cooked, add the mussels and clams to the pan. Cook for a few minutes until the shells have opened up (discard any that remain closed), then turn the heat off. Remove the octopus to a board, discard the skin and suckers, the brown meat from inside the head, the beak, and the eye, and slice the head up. Roughly slice the tentacles at an angle. Correct the seasoning of the broth in the pan, then divide it between 6 bowls. Divide the octopus, mussels, and clams between the bowls, sprinkle the fennel tops and parsley over all, and drizzle with extra virgin olive oil. PS, This is lovely with some cooked white beans added to it.

spiedini di polpo *octopus kebabs*

serves 6

1 tender octopus (see page 180)
juice of 1 lemon
1 fresh red chili, chopped

a small bunch of fresh flat-leaf parsley,
 leaves picked and chopped

Remove the cooked octopus to a board and cut off the tentacles. Discard the brown meat from inside the head, the beak, and the eye, and slice the head up. Wind the tentacles and meat up like pinwheels and thread them onto skewers (if using wooden ones soak them in water first). Grill on a barbecue, squeezing over a little lemon juice when you turn them. Serve on a platter with some chopped fresh red chili and parsley leaves.

insalata di polpo *octopus salad*

serves 6

1 tender octopus (see page 180)
a handful of mussels, cleaned and
 debearded
a small handful of fresh flat-leaf parsley
2 carrots, peeled and sliced into very fine
 matchsticks

2 sticks of celery, sliced into very
 fine matchsticks
½ a bulb of fennel, sliced into very fine
 matchsticks, herby tops reserved
olive oil
good herb vinegar

When the octopus is nearly cooked, add your mussels to the pan, cook for a few minutes more, until the shells have opened up (discard any that remain closed), then turn the heat off. Slice your parsley and put it into a large bowl with your carrot, celery, and fennel. Remove the octopus to a board, remove the skin and suckers, and roughly slice the tentacles at an angle. Remove and discard the brown meat from inside the head, the beak, and the eye, and slice the head up. Remove your mussels from their shells and toss with the octopus slices and the vegetables. Dress with 2 good glugs of olive oil, a few swigs of herb vinegar, and a little of the cooking liquor. Season to taste and sprinkle the chopped fennel tops over all.

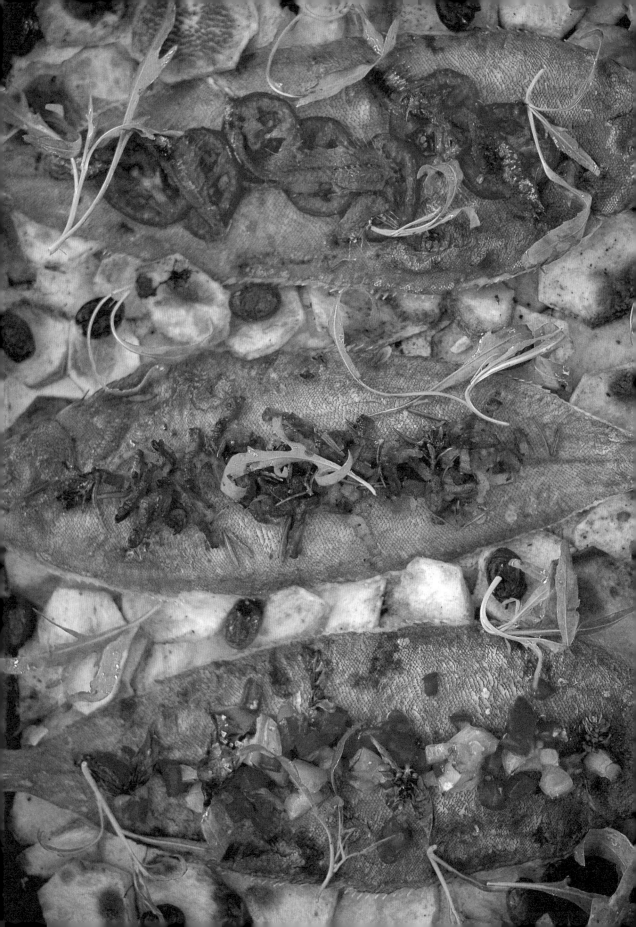

sogliola in tre modi

serves 4

roasted sole three ways

Dover and lemon sole are lovely when roasted and topped with flavorings like smoky pancetta and rosemary, or sweet tomatoes and balsamic vinegar. When cooked with these flavors on a layer of potatoes, a simple dish is taken to another dimension. The finished dish looks fantastic, and the best thing is that you can make it look like a completely different dinner each week simply by changing your topping! The soles I've come across in Italy are generally cooked whole, and are taken straight to the table where everyone can reach over and help themselves. The lovely white flesh will pull easily away from the bones. Cooked whole like this, the fish is much more juicy and tasty.

PS, In the picture I've used my three favorite toppings. All you have to do is choose which one you want to go for – the quantities I've given for each topping will make enough to cover your four fish.

8 medium potatoes, peeled
olive oil
a handful of fresh rosemary, leaves
 picked
a handful of black olives, pitted
sea salt and freshly ground black pepper
4 Dover or lemon soles, scaled and
 trimmed
extra virgin olive oil
juice of 1 lemon
a handful of wild arugula

topping choices
4 ripe red tomatoes, sliced
8 anchovy fillets, sliced into strips
or
12 slices of pancetta, chopped
4 sprigs of fresh rosemary, leaves picked
or
20 red and yellow cherry tomatoes, deseeded
 and roughly chopped
4 sprigs of fresh basil, leaves picked
 and torn

Preheat the oven to 400°F and select a roasting pan just big enough to hold all your fish side by side in one layer.

Slice the potatoes about ½ inch thick, toss with a little olive oil, add the rosemary, olives, salt, and pepper, and spread out evenly, in one layer, in the roasting pan. Cover the pan tightly with a double-thickness layer of aluminum foil and bake in the preheated oven for 20 minutes, or until the potatoes are just soft. Remove the foil and return the pan to the oven for 10 minutes, until the potatoes are lightly golden.

Brush the soles with a little olive oil and season them lightly with salt and pepper. Remove the pan from the oven and lay the fish side by side on top of the hot potatoes. Take your chosen topping ingredients and sprinkle them over the fish. Drizzle with a little extra virgin olive oil and return the pan to the oven for 15–20 minutes, until the fish is cooked and lightly golden.

To serve, either scatter over a little olive-oil-and-lemon-dressed arugula or have a mixed salad on the side. And maybe have some extra lemon wedges for squeezing over.

calamari in padella con limone e pangrattato

serves 4 as a starter, 2 as a main

pan-fried squid with lemons and pangrattato

I found a recipe similar to this in an old Italian cookbook. In a funny sort of way, it's a bit like fish and chips because you have a lovely contrast between the tender soft texture of the squid and the crunchy pangrattato, which is similar to a batter. It's a similar combo of textures and tastes, with an extra kick of chili and the zinginess of the lemon. Great to make if you have some stale breadcrumbs around.

olive oil
1–2 fresh red chilies, pricked
6 cloves of garlic, unpeeled,
  lightly crushed
2 large handfuls of stale breadcrumbs
sea salt and freshly ground black pepper

4 baby squid, trimmed and cleaned
  (wings left on, tentacles left whole)
½ a lemon, very thinly sliced
a handful of flat-leaf parsley, leaves
  picked and sliced

To make your *pangrattato,* put 6 tablespoons of oil into a thick-bottomed pan. Add the whole chilies, garlic, and breadcrumbs and stir for a couple of minutes, until the breadcrumbs are crisp and golden. Season with a little salt and pepper and drain on paper towels.

Wipe the pan with paper towels and put it back on a high heat. Add a good splash of oil, then season the squid and tentacles and lay them gently in the hot pan with the lemon slices. If you can't fit them all in, cook them in two batches – you don't want them all cramped together. Fry for a minute or so, until golden, then turn the squid over and fry for the same amount of time on the other side. The lemons will color and need to be turned quicker than the squid, so just remove them from the pan and put to one side when they look like the ones in the picture. Small squid should be cooked through in this time, but if your squid are larger they'll need a bit longer. Take the pan off the heat and divide the squid and lemon slices between your plates. Scatter the *pangrattato* and the finely sliced parsley over the top of the squid. Great served with a lightly dressed arugula salad and a glass of cold white wine.

pesce alla griglia
grilled fish

One night in Palermo I found myself grilling fish with the "grill man" in Il Borgo night market. Just to put it into context, this isn't the safest place to be at night – to me it seemed like the nearest thing to modern-day anarchy, with twelve-year-olds driving around in beaten-up cars and six-year-olds on scooters, often with a two-year-old passenger! The night I was there, a mother, along with her daughter and grandmother, was giving her son-in-law a bashing because he had been unfaithful and there was a lot of general shouting! It's a very atmospheric place and is the heart of street food in Sicily.

What happens at Il Borgo is that you buy your fish from a nearby fishmonger – they're all pretty exceptional and the fish is sublime – then you give the grill man a couple of euros and he cooks it for you with some oil and salt. You stand around and have a drink while he's cooking, then you stand around while you eat, and after that you continue standing around just watching everything that's going on! I came up with some very simple ways of flavoring the grilled fish using fresh and dried herbs, flavored salt, and flavored oil which, when either stuffed into or brushed, rubbed, and sprinkled on the fish while it's grilling, give an absolutely fantastic flavor. I like to grab a bunch of rosemary, thyme, bay, or oregano, or a mixture, tie it up tightly with string, and use it to brush the oil onto the fish. The locals really only cook their fish plainly – they don't flavor it with anything at all as it's so fresh. Although they're not really up for trying new things, when I gave this simply flavored fish to them they went crazy for it and thought it was fantastic!

By flavoring the oil and salt you get subtle, fragrant tastes, so next time you do a barbecue try using this method – you won't regret it. It also works well with things like chicken, legs of lamb, and pork chops, so feel free to try, say, roast chicken rubbed with *salmoriglio* or a pork chop seasoned with orange and rosemary salt (see page 194 for both recipes).

My favorite fresh herb is fennel, but things like parsley, basil, and mint, finely sliced, stuffed into the cavity of your fish and into slashes on the outside, can give the most incredible perfume. The skin goes crispy but the herbs inside will be steaming and perfuming the flesh – an absolute joy. The four herbs I've mentioned above are very delicate in flavor, and you would have to be far too generous with the amounts to overwhelm the flavor of most fish. Scatter the flavored orange and rosemary salt over shrimp or fish like red mullet as well – absolutely delicious.

my thoughts on barbecues

If you have a choice of which barbecue to buy, go for a heavy-duty one with big thick bars. Caribbean Cookers (www.caribbeancookers.com) are the only ones I use now – they're not all that cheap but you'll never regret buying one. I came across them in Oxford where they are built in the owners' garage! Twenty years down the line they'll still be as good, and will look even better.

my thoughts on lighting the fire

When you're next clearing up the garden, don't throw away any twigs or sticks. Put them in the garage or shed to dry – once lit they'll burn really quickly. I think lighter fluid and sprays leave a lingering taste which is horrible (plus, one of my friends once set himself alight when spraying a barbecue with gasoline . . .). Small bits of dried wood and leaves, scrunched-up bits of newspaper, charcoal, and a bit of blowing make the perfect combination.

First of all, make sure your barbecue is clean and the air vents underneath are open. Put a layer of scrunched-up paper in first, then crisscross your kindling like a little tepee so you have plenty of gaps for air. Next, put a few small pieces of charcoal around, then some more bits of paper and kindling. Build the material up about one foot high and then light it at the base, at each side, back, and front. Rip off a piece of sturdy cardboard and use that to fan the fire.

After 10 minutes it should be going well, so keep fanning and let it do its own thing. As the charcoal gets whiter and hotter, add another layer but don't just dump a load on top or the fire will go out. Once you've got a generous amount of charcoal chugging away, keep one side high, almost touching the bars, sloping down to the other side. Then let the fire simmer down till it's white hot and the flames have gone – this will take anything from thirty minutes to an hour, depending on the size of your charcoal. A friend of mine has a small secondary barbecue he calls a "hot box," which he keeps extra hot charcoal in – so he can top up when cooking for over fifteen people.

my thoughts on grilling fish

Get yourself a mixture of large whole fish – cod, grouper, sea bass, even a smaller flounder or turbot – as these are fantastic. And filleted fish as well, things like red mullet, snapper, or sea bream. Squid and little sardines are absolutely delicious too. Some people are scared to cook fish as they are worried about undercooking it, but if you're using fresh fish put your paranoia on the other side and worry about overcooking it. To tell if a fish is cooked, I can give you some rough directions, but it really depends on your barbecue and how hot it is. Grilling fish is one of the easiest things to do, as the food isn't hidden away in the oven. It's right in front of you – you can see it, hear it, smell it. You're in control. Before you start cooking, rub the bars with a little oil on a rag – this will stop the fish sticking to them. Another trick I learned in Italy is that if you season your fish well, and put it to one side for fifteen minutes before cooking, it won't stick to the bars because the salt removes water from the skin. Very clever.

If you've got a whole bunch of different fish – big, small, fat, thin, whole or filleted – they're all going to take different times to cook. Obviously if a fish is big and on the bone it might need half an hour on the cooler end of the barbecue or even have to be finished off in the oven; but if it's something small, like an anchovy, or filleted, like red mullet, it will take no time at all on the hot side. Lay your fish out on a pan before you start cooking, arranged in order from longest cooking time to shortest. If you're using flavorings, get them made and ready.

(continued on page 194)

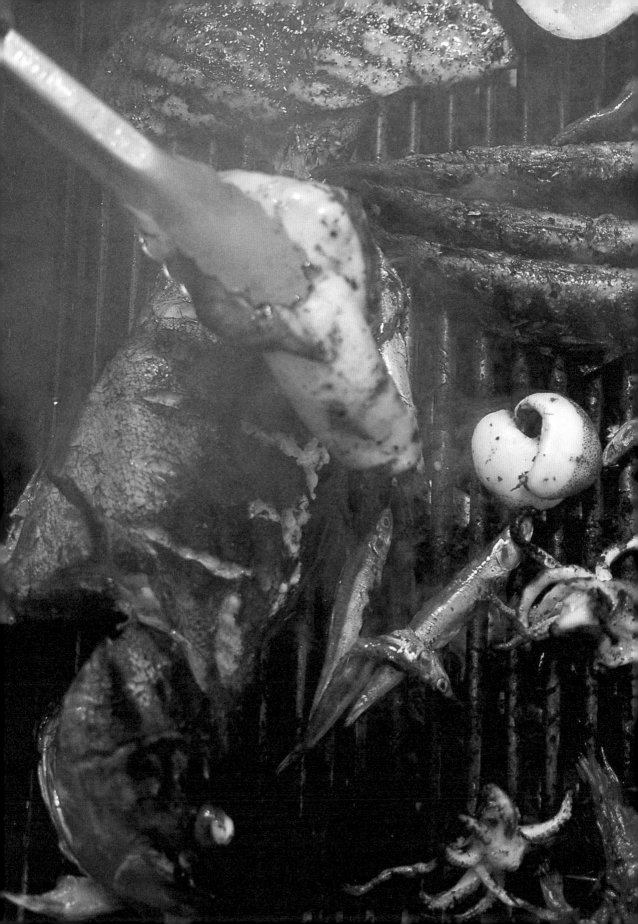

On a hot barbie any fillet of fish about a half inch thick will require only a couple of minutes on each side to be beautifully cooked. If twice as thick, cook for twice as long – just use your common sense. You can always poke your knife into the thickest part to see if it's cooked. If you're cooking fish on the bone you need to start it off hot and then put it to one side to finish off – when the flesh pulls away from the bone it's cooked. Things like shrimp and scallops are always lovely, and you can skewer them to keep them together. I try to use one flavoring for each particular kind of fish, so that each one is a totally different experience.

Once the fish is cooked, drizzle it with olive oil and a squeeze of lemon juice and put it all on a platter in the middle of the table. A few finger bowls with warm water and sliced lemon are always nice to put around the table when you're going to be getting your fingers dirty.

salmoriglio (marjoram sauce)

Put 2 handfuls of fresh marjoram or oregano into a pestle and mortar and smash and grind to a paste. Loosen well with extra virgin olive oil. Squeeze in some lemon juice, taste it, and season with salt and pepper. If you think more lemon juice is needed, feel free to add it. This oil is exceptionally good rubbed or brushed on fish before grilling, or after it has finished cooking. It's great with tuna and swordfish in particular, and it also goes really well with chicken and white meat.

rosemary and orange salt

You've got to try this flavored salt – you won't believe how zingy it tastes. Make sure you use finely ground sea salt – not table salt. In Sicily they are quite generous with the amount of salt they use – just rub your chosen amount on fish or meat, pat with olive oil, and grill it. You can also use it to rub on pork, or to sprinkle over tomato salad with a little basil. Or on pan-fried shrimp . . .

2 good sprigs of fresh rosemary,   zest of 1 lemon
  leaves picked   3½ oz. (6 good tablespoons) ground sea salt
zest of 1 orange

In a pestle and mortar, or a food processor, bash up the rosemary leaves to a pulp. Using a fine grater, preferably one of those Microplane or Cuisipro ones, finely zest the orange and lemon, and add to the rosemary. Mix the salt with the rosemary mixture, using your fingers, and lay it out on a tray – it will be damp and muddy but will become harder as it dries out. You can use it at once or let it dry for 5 or 6 hours and break it up with your hands before using. It keeps for a month or so in an airtight jar.

pesce spada alla griglia con la salsa di giovanna

grilled swordfish with salsa di giovanna

Anna Tasca Lanza runs the Regaleali estate in Sicily and is one of the most renowned cooks in Italy. Giovanna is the backbone of her kitchen, and this sauce is one of her specialities. She uses it with fish – it's fantastic with large fish like tuna, swordfish, and shark but is also wonderful thrown into a pan with things like squid and shrimp. To be honest, if you smeared it all over a chicken before roasting it you'd do yourself pretty proud too.

juice of 1 lemon
extra virgin olive oil
sea salt and freshly ground black pepper
3 cloves of garlic, peeled and finely sliced
a sprig of fresh mint, leaves picked and
  roughly sliced

a sprig of fresh oregano, leaves picked and
  roughly sliced
4 ½-inch-thick slices of swordfish
  or tuna

Squeeze the lemon juice into a bowl and add 3 times the amount of olive oil. Season with salt and pepper and stir in the garlic, mint, and oregano.

Heat a griddle pan or frying pan until very hot and season your swordfish or tuna with salt and pepper. Place it in the pan and cook for around a minute on each side, until golden. This will leave the fish slightly pink in the middle, so if you don't like the idea of this, feel free to cook it a little more. Divide the fish between your serving plates and spoon the sauce over the top.

secondi | fish 197

trapani market in sicily –
famous for tuna and sardines

pesce intero al forno in crosta di sale

serves 6–8

whole fish baked in salt

The southern Italians often cook fish whole, especially baked in salt. The basic principle is to pack salt around the whole fish before baking, whether it's a whole sea bass or turbot or tuna (as in the picture) or smaller fish like sardines. Any whole fish can be baked in salt, but you have to gut it first. The other thing to bear in mind is that you don't want the salt to get into any exposed parts of the fish – the salt is not used for seasoning, it's part of the cooking method. What happens is that when the salt goes into the oven it bakes hard like pottery, giving you really dry and crispy fish on the outside while retaining the juices and natural flavors on the inside.

The basic way to make a salt crust is to add water to salt (always use sea salt) and pack it all around the fish. With little bream, mullet, or sardines you can keep the salt ½ inch thick, but if you move on to a 7-lb. sea bass, for example, you need to end up with 1¼ inches of salt around it. I've improved my old way of doing it by adding an egg to make an even harder baking case. I'm also adding fennel seeds and lemon and orange peel to infuse a lovely subtle flavor. PS, You may think this sounds like a bit of a bother but it really is very easy.

4½ lb. fish (see above), scaled and gutted
a few sprigs of fresh herbs (basil, parsley, herby fennel tops)
2 lemons, 1 sliced and 1 zested
7 lb. coarse sea salt (for every 1–1¼ lb. fish you need 3½ lb. salt)
zest of 1 orange
1 egg, preferably organic, beaten
a handful of fennel seeds
olive oil

Preheat the oven to 425°F. After your fish has been gutted, stuff the cavity with a mixture of nice herbs and aromatics such as basil, parsley, herby fennel tops, and slices of lemon. Mix the salt with the orange and lemon zest, egg, and fennel seeds. Pour in a few splashes of water and scrunch the mix together until it looks like wet sand. Sprinkle about ½ inch of the salt in a baking pan, making a little bed for each fish. Rub the fish skin with oil and place the fish on top of the salt. Pour the rest of the salt on top, patting it down. You don't have to worry about covering the head and tail.

Bake the fish in the preheated oven for 20 to 40 minutes. The timing does depend, however, on the thickness of the salt, your oven, the type and size of fish you're using, and the temperature of the fish when it went into the oven. It's hard to be 100 percent accurate, so the best thing to do is prod a fork into the thickest part of the fish, hold it there for 10 seconds, then pull it out quickly and rest the prongs on your lip. If the prongs feel warm, the fish is cooked, and if not, it needs longer. If you're still not sure, pull a bit of the salt away and check to see if the flesh pulls away from the bone. If it doesn't, pop it back in the oven. Serve at the table, breaking open the salt in front of your guests. (It's handy to have another bowl nearby to put the salt into.)

le migliori polpette di tonno

the best tuna meatballs

serves 4

Just about everyone I know is a fan of meatballs, so I thought I'd give you a recipe for these, as they are something a little different. I've seen them made in Sicily in the same way, using a mixture of swordfish and tuna – not canned tuna though. These have to be made with fresh fish and they are subtly seasoned with Sicilian herbs and spices – this recipe is just as good as the meat versions!

for the tomato sauce
olive oil
1 small onion, peeled and finely chopped
4 cloves of garlic, peeled and finely sliced
1 teaspoon dried oregano
2 14-oz. cans of good-quality
   plum tomatoes
sea salt and freshly ground black pepper
red wine vinegar
a small bunch of fresh flat-leaf parsley,
   leaves picked and roughly chopped

for the meatballs
14 oz. tuna
olive oil
2 oz. pinenuts
1 level teaspoon ground cinnamon
sea salt and freshly ground black pepper
1 teaspoon dried oregano
a handful of fresh flat-leaf parsley, chopped
1¾ cups stale breadcrumbs
2 oz. freshly grated Parmesan
2 eggs
zest and juice of 1 lemon

First make your sauce. Place a large pan on the heat, add a good glug of olive oil, your onion and garlic, and fry slowly for 10 or so minutes, until soft. Add your oregano, the tomatoes, salt, and pepper and bring to a boil. Simmer for 15 minutes or so, then blend until smooth. Taste – it might need a tiny swig of red wine vinegar or some extra seasoning.

While the tomatoes are simmering, chop the tuna up into 1-inch dice. Pour a good couple of tablespoons of olive oil into a large frying pan and place on the heat. Add the tuna to the pan with the pinenuts and cinnamon. Season lightly with salt and pepper and fry for a minute or so to cook the tuna on all sides and toast the pinenuts. Remove from the heat and put the mixture into a bowl. Allow to cool down for 5 minutes, then add the oregano, parsley, breadcrumbs, Parmesan, eggs, lemon zest, and juice to the bowl. Using your hands, really scrunch and mix the flavors into the tuna, then divide the mixture and squeeze it into meatballs slightly smaller than a golf ball. If you dip one of your hands in water while shaping, you'll get a nice smooth surface on the meatball. If the mixture's very sticky, add a few more breadcrumbs. Keep the meatballs around the same size and place them on an oiled tray, then put them in the fridge for an hour to let them rest.

Put the pan you fried the tuna in back on the heat with a little olive oil. Add your meatballs to the pan and jiggle them about until they're golden brown all over. You might want to do them in batches – when they're done, add them to the tomato sauce, divide between your plates, sprinkle with chopped parsley, and drizzle with good olive oil. Great served with spaghetti or linguine.

tonno di nonna fangitta

serves 4

nonna fangitta's tuna

A lovely lady called Nonna Fangitta made me this incredible dish on the island of Favignana off the coast of Sicily. It's so so good, and any leftovers can be used in pasta or in a salad the next day. Make sure you get your tuna in a whole piece, rather than in bits.

1 lb. 2 oz. fresh, ripe tomatoes (red,
  yellow, and orange if you can get them)
14 oz. fresh tuna fillet, whole
3 cloves of garlic, peeled and finely sliced
2 sprigs of fresh rosemary, leaves picked
1 fresh red chili, deseeded and
  finely sliced
olive oil
a small handful of capers, rinsed

6 anchovy fillets
1 heaping teaspoon dried oregano
1 cinnamon stick
1 14-oz. can of good-quality plum tomatoes
sea salt and freshly ground black pepper
optional: extra virgin olive oil
optional: a small handful of fresh flat-leaf
  parsley, chopped

Get a pot that snugly fits your tuna – it's important that you don't use one that's too big, because you want to poach the tuna in the tomato sauce. If the pot is too big it won't work, because the sauce won't cover the tuna. Put your pot on a high heat and add a kettleful of boiling water. Put the tomatoes into the water for about 40 seconds, and drain them in a colander. Remove them to a bowl of cold water for 30 seconds, then set aside and allow to cool a little before rubbing the skin off, removing the cores, and carefully squeezing out the seeds. Meanwhile, carefully stab one side of the tuna at an angle about 8 or 9 times. In each incision (as you can see in the picture), place a slice of garlic, a little sprig of rosemary, and a sliver of chili. (Any leftover garlic, rosemary, and chili will be used in the tomato sauce.)

Put the pot back on the heat and add a little olive oil. Add the remaining garlic, chili, and rosemary with the capers, anchovies, oregano, and cinnamon stick and cook gently until the garlic softens. Add the tomatoes, together with the canned tomatoes, bring to a boil, then lower the heat to a gentle simmer. Break up the tomatoes in the sauce with a wooden spoon and season with salt and pepper. Carefully add the tuna to the sauce, pushing it right down so that the sauce completely covers it. Place the lid on the pot, slightly ajar, and simmer for around 25 minutes (depending on the thickness of your tuna). You can test to see how cooked it is by removing it from the sauce and seeing if it flakes.

Once cooked, take the pot off the heat and let it cool down to eating temperature with the lid on. In Italy, you'd normally eat this as a fish course with a drizzle of extra virgin olive oil and some parsley scattered over, but it would also be good on crostini. I like to serve it in the pot in the middle of the table so that people can help themselves. Lovely with some bread.

couscous con pesce di nonna giusy

serves 4

nonna giusy's fish with couscous

When I was on the island of Marettimo I found out that it's famous for its African-influenced couscous dishes. I walked around the town one day asking the locals who made the best couscous, and, of course, every answer was "Mia mama!" That is, until one lad took me along to meet his grandmother – Nonna Giusy. She was the most incredible woman, who made her own couscous by hand, using coarse semolina flour and rubbing it in a bowl with a bit of water until it stuck together in little chunky bits. It was so delicious, and incredibly easy to make, but I think the type of flour she was using will be hard to find outside Italy so I would suggest using quality bought couscous instead.

This is how the women on the island prepare whatever fish their husbands catch at sea each day. When they see the boats coming in they put the couscous on to steam and get ready to start poaching the fish. It's a really interesting method and damn tasty. I was at Nonna Giusy's house for three hours learning how to make it, so thanks, Nonna! (And she makes a mean limoncello too!)

for the couscous
1 small onion, peeled
½ a bulb of garlic, peeled
a large handful of fresh flat-leaf parsley,
  leaves picked
14 oz. couscous

for the fish
olive oil
1 large white onion, peeled and sliced

4 cloves of garlic, peeled and sliced
½ a dried red chili, crumbled
2 11–14-oz. red mullet or bream, gutted and
  scaled
2 1½ lb jars of stewed tomatoes
sea salt and freshly ground black pepper
a large handful of fresh flat-leaf
  parsley, chopped

To make the couscous, put the onion, garlic, and parsley into a food processor and whiz up until fine. Mix with the couscous, then put into a steamer or use a colander over a pan of boiling water and let it steam very slowly for half an hour. Transfer to a serving bowl.

Meanwhile, put a pan on a low heat and add a good glug of olive oil. Add the sliced onion and garlic and the chili and cook gently for about 5 minutes. Add the fish to the pan, then pour in the stewed tomatoes and the same amount of water so that the fish is covered. Season with a little salt and pepper and simmer gently for 20 minutes. Remove from the heat and carefully transfer the fish to a plate, then pour half the sauce into the bowl of couscous and mix together. At this point Nonna Giusy placed a couple of towels over the bowl so the couscous remained warm while it absorbed the sauce. You can do this, or cover the bowl with aluminium foil and place in a very low oven (160°F) for 30 minutes.

Flake the meat from the fish and put into a second serving bowl. Be careful to remove all the bones. Pour the rest of the poaching sauce over the top, sprinkle with chopped parsley, and serve with the bowl of couscous in the middle of the table for people to help themselves.

meat

I'm highly aware that the picture opposite is both graphic and gruesome, so I'm going to explain why I decided to use it in the book and also why this whole chapter is quite visually gritty. This was an incredibly normal sight in Italy. I felt strongly about using it because I found that when I spoke to Italians about their meat, most of the time they would tell me about the natural surroundings in which the animal had lived and what it had eaten throughout its life, foraging for lovely herbs and chestnuts and fruits, and about how it was treated. All this before they'd even slaughtered it or thought about cooking it for themselves. There seems to be a real understanding, even from kids, that some animals are for food and are certainly not kept as pets. I love the fact that their concept of humane does not just relate to the slaughter but goes all the way back through the whole life of the animal and its welfare.

It was important for me to show this in the book, because it's an honest reflection of what I saw in Italy, and also because far too many people in Britain and the U.S. choose to close the door on these uncomfortable aspects of eating meat. And for me, therein lies the problem. Because the majority of people don't want to see the dead animal that their cut of meat is coming from, big corporations have jumped in to solve the problem – out of sight, out of mind. Animals are battery-farmed in disturbing conditions and pumped full of antibiotics (because disease is so rife in the confines that they live in). And, of course, they can then offer you a mass-produced leg or breast of chicken, or they'll try to help you feed your kids by processing, reformulating, reshaping, and repackaging meat so it's unrecognizable. With a cocktail of additives and preservatives, colorings, and flavor enhancers in food, it's not hard to realize why Britain is one of the unhealthiest countries in Europe and why my kids' generation is the first to be expected to die before their parents. How completely shocking is that?

For most of his life the shepherd in this picture has earned less than a British person on the dole, but the meat he eats is as good as anything served to royalty. It's the honesty between the average Italian and the land which is one of the things that help them to make the right choice in their diets – it's this that has allowed them to become the third longest-living country in the world, after Japan and Iceland.

As you can tell, this issue is something I feel very strongly about. I also hope you look at this picture, and a couple of others in this chapter, slightly differently now from how you might have done before reading this. And, after this, if you still want to be a vegetarian, I salute you. But if you want to eat good meat then I really do salute you! We're at the top of the food chain, after all. But for goodness' sake, please stop supporting these w*****s that produce cheap, tasteless food, which is more unnatural than you would ever believe. Do me a favor and go to my website, www.jamieoliver.com, and click on the link for The Meatrix. It's an incredible little film with a very strong message and is something you can show your kids.

And next time you buy some meat, it really should be free-range or organic. If you can't afford this six or seven days a week, cut your losses and have it three or four times a week instead, like the Italians do – quality not quantity. And most importantly, ask your butcher where the animal comes from, what it's been fed on, and how it's been treated. That's a good place to start.

peposo

the famous hunter's peppery beef stew

This is an amazingly powerful old Tuscan dish. Don't be put off by the amount of garlic and pepper – it's no hotter than a mild curry, and has a fantastic flavor. Try cooking it overnight in a low oven and it will be meltingly soft and delicious by morning. It's also known as the "hunter's brunch," as it's great hearty food after a morning spent hunting. When eaten on bruschette (as in the picture), it's energy on toast!

I've seen this dish made with the meat and bone sliced through, a bit like an osso bucco. Some butchers won't do this for you, so what I've done here is to get the shin home, then slice the meat off it into thick slices. The bone can be thrown in for flavor and the results are really authentic.

5½ lb. beef or veal shin, on the bone
20 garlic cloves, peeled
4 heaping tablespoons freshly ground
  black pepper

sea salt
5 sprigs of fresh rosemary
2 bottles of Chianti or other fruity red wine
2 bay leaves

Slice your meat into chunky slabs and get it all off the bone. Preheat the oven to 300°F. Get yourself a large pan, just big enough to hold all the ingredients. Place a layer of your sliced meat at the bottom of the pan, cover with a few whole cloves of garlic, then sprinkle well with one of your tablespoons of pepper and a little salt. Add a sprig or two of rosemary, then repeat with another layer of beef and keep layering the ingredients like this until they're used up and the pot is almost full. Pour the wine over the top, add the bone and the bay leaves, and top up with water if necessary to cover the meat.

Bring to a boil, cover tightly with a double-thickness layer of aluminum foil, and place in the preheated oven for 6 hours or until tender. If you want to cook the stew overnight (as many Italians do), lower the oven temp to 275°F and it can cook for 8 hours or more, until the meat is tender and falling apart. Make sure the foil is well sealed, as this will keep all the moisture inside the pot.

When the stew's done, take the foil off, skim off any fat from the surface of the stew, and remove the bone, the bay leaves, and the rosemary twigs. The meat should be really soft and the juice light but rich and powerful in flavor. Taste and season if you think it needs it. Then break the meat up with a spoon and serve a ladleful of the stew on a hot toasted bruschetta with a drizzle of oil – a wonderful warming brunch on a cold winter's morning. Or serve simply with boiled carrots, new potatoes, and cavolo nero or kale as a more complete dinner. Would also be lovely with some polenta and a drizzle of good-quality extra virgin olive oil.

maiale alla griglia e arrosto

grilled and roasted pork

serves 12

When I was in Altamura, in Puglia, I cooked this grilled and roasted pork loin with a group of Italian friends. It's a great thing to serve at a party because when you've grilled it on all sides for fifteen minutes you can just pop it into a hot oven for an hour quite happily and leave it – and you can serve it as a hot roast or have it cold. My boss at the River Café, Rose Gray, used to baste her grilled pork with herb vinegar and bay leaves, which was a tremendous combination, so feel free to do this, or to use rosemary instead of bay. The way we flavored ours in Italy was with fennel seeds, dried chili, salt, and pepper. I'm going to give you the recipe for twelve, but feel free to halve it, or even double it. It's dead simple, and it's made even easier if you ask your butcher to prepare the meat for you. Just ask for a 4½-lb. loin of pork, off the bone with the skin removed.

2 heaping tablespoons fennel seeds
2 or 3 dried red chilies
1 4½-lb. pork loin, preferably organic
  (see above)

olive oil
sea salt and freshly ground black pepper
10 tablespoons good-quality red wine vinegar
a bunch of fresh rosemary, leaves picked

First of all, smash your fennel seeds up in a pestle and mortar and crumble and bash in your dried chili – now, this is supposed to give a subtle heat, so I'm going to leave it up to you to use as much or as little as you prefer. Put your loin of pork onto a cutting board and score the fat in a crisscross fashion. Rub the meat all over with a little olive oil, then sprinkle the fennel seeds and chili all over the pork. Cover the pork up and put it to one side in a roasting pan – if it has come straight out of the fridge, let it come to room temperature – so that it can absorb the flavors.

About an hour before you're ready to cook, you need to light your barbecue and get it to the right temperature (see my notes on page 191). I'd advise you to use charcoal instead of gas so that you get a lovely chargrilled flavor coming through. You can also, of course, roast the meat in the oven, but I prefer to do it on the barbecue. (If you roast it in the oven for the whole time, it'll need 1 hour 20 minutes.) Either way, season the meat quite generously with salt and pepper and place it fat-side-down on the grill. This will make the barbecue flame a bit so you'll probably need to turn it over quickly onto the meat side, but it does tend to get the bars oiled up and the smoke going, which we like. Grill the meat for 10–15 minutes, depending on how hot your barbecue is, and remember to keep turning it so it gets those lovely charred bar marks all over it.

Remove the pork to the same roasting pan you marinated it in and put it into the oven at 400°F. After half an hour add the vinegar and rosemary leaves, carefully move the meat around and baste it, and put it back into the oven for another 20 minutes. Remove it from the oven, leave it to rest for 10 minutes, then slice the meat up. All the lovely juices from the pan can be kept warm and poured over the meat just before serving. If you've been to Italy, you may have noticed that you really do just get some slices of meat with a simple side dish. At the end of the day, the meat tastes great; so serve it in any way you see fit.

deboning a pig in tuscany to roast it
whole in the wood oven behind me

spiedini di salsiccia e manzo

serves 4

sausage and beef kebabs

This is an incredibly simple, gutsy, authentic Italian kebab. You can swap the beef for pork or the pancetta for good smoked bacon, but if you start swapping amazing Italian sausages for any cheap old sausage, you might as well not bother making it. Italian sausages are plump, coarsely ground, and have cured meat in them, but if you can't get them, a good-quality meaty Cumberland will be very acceptable. You may find that when you pinch and twist the sausages they splurge out of the ends, but don't worry. If you can't get your butcher to slice your bacon thickly, simply roll up slices of normal bacon and skewer them. For skewering you can use wooden sticks (soaked in water first) or metal skewers, or get some long rosemary sprigs – have a look around on your walk home from work because rosemary bushes are everywhere (it's not stealing, it's pruning!).

You can barbecue these kebabs, but the easiest way is to roast them in the oven. Great served with a big plate of polenta, and if you're not familiar with polenta this is the opportunity to try making it (see page 269).

12 1-inch cubes of beef fillet or pork	2 cloves of garlic, peeled
4 large good-quality Italian or Cumberland sausages	1 lemon, zested and halved extra virgin olive oil
4 thickly sliced pieces of pancetta or bacon	sea salt and freshly ground black pepper
18 fresh sage leaves	4 long, firm sprigs of fresh rosemary (or use skewers)

First of all, you need to marinate your meat, so put your pieces of beef into a bowl. Get your sausages and gently twist and pinch each one to give you three smaller round sausages, then use a knife or scissors to cut them apart and add them to the bowl. Slice your pancetta or bacon into 1-inch pieces – you should get 4 or 5 out of each slice – and add to the bowl. Put 12 of your sage leaves into the bowl and bash the rest up with the garlic cloves and lemon zest using a pestle and mortar, or a metal bowl with a rolling pin, until you have a pulp. Drizzle in about 4 tablespoons of extra virgin olive oil and the juice of half the lemon. Stir well and pour over the meat in the bowl. It's best to leave this to marinate for 1–3 hours in the fridge, but you can cook the meat straight away if you don't have time.

Preheat the oven to its highest setting. Now you want to make your spiedini. If you're using rosemary sprigs, remove all the leaves apart from a few at the top. I usually keep the leaves for cooking something else. Scratch your knife down the stick to remove the bark, then cut the end of the stick at an angle so it can be used to "spear" the food. If you're using proper wooden kebab sticks or metal skewers it will obviously be slightly easier, but it won't taste quite as nice. Now all you need to do is skewer each of the kebabs, starting with a piece of pancetta, then a folded sage leaf, then a piece of sausage, and finally a cube of beef. Do this three times for each skewer, finishing with a piece of pancetta. Put the kebabs onto an oiled tray or pan and place in the oven. Immediately turn it down to 400°F – this will give you a nice roasting start, and as the heat lowers a little it will make the meat nice and juicy. Roast for about 20 minutes, until the sausages are golden. Squeeze over the remaining lemon juice and serve.

salsicce con lenticchie verdi e salsa di pomodoro

sausages and green lentils with tomato salsa

The equivalent of bangers and mash in Italy is definitely a good roasted sausage with a pile of lenticchie di Castelluccio and a spicy salsa rossa tomato sauce – a genius combo.

8 medium-sized good-quality Italian
  sausages, or good fat Cumberlands
olive oil
1 lb., 2oz purple-sprouting broccoli
  or cima di rapa
juice of ½ a lemon
extra virgin olive oil
sea salt and freshly ground black pepper
a small handful of fresh thyme tips

for the salsa rossa
olive oil
1 small red onion, peeled and finely
  chopped
3 cloves of garlic, peeled and finely sliced

1 small stick of cinnamon
1–2 small dried red chilies, crumbled
2 tablespoons red wine vinegar, plus
  extra for dressing
2 14-oz. cans of good-quality plum tomatoes
for the lentils
14 oz. lenticchie di Castelluccio or
  Puy lentils
2 cloves of garlic, peeled
1 bay leaf
a handful of fresh flat-leaf parsley, leaves
  chopped, stems reserved
red wine vinegar or sherry vinegar

First things first; get your salsa on the go. Put a little olive oil into a pan, add the onion and sliced garlic, throw in the cinnamon stick and a good crumbling of chili, and fry on a gentle heat for 10 minutes, until the onions are soft and sweet. Now turn the heat up and add your red wine vinegar – it will steam and might even make you cough but this is a normal reaction! Then turn the heat down to low and add your canned tomatoes, chopped up. Simmer slowly for half an hour while you get on with your lentils.

Preheat the oven to 400°F. Put the lentils into a pot, cover them with water, and add the 2 whole cloves of garlic, the bay leaf, and some tied-up stems from the parsley. Simmer for around 20 minutes, making sure that you've got enough liquid covering the lentils. Toss your sausages in a little olive oil and put them in a roasting pan in the preheated oven for 25 minutes or until golden and crisp. Drop your broccoli into a pot of boiling water for a few minutes when the sausages come out of the oven. When done, drain in a colander and toss in a bowl with a squeeze of lemon juice and some extra virgin olive oil.

Once the lentils are cooked, remove the parsley stems and bay leaf and pour away most of the water from the pot. Mash the garlic cloves up with a spoon, mix in with the lentils, and dress them using 4 tablespoons of good extra virgin olive oil and 1 or 2 tablespoons of good vinegar. Throw in all your finely chopped parsley leaves, mix, and season.

Remove the sausages from the roasting pan and pour away any fat. Tip the lentils into your serving bowls. Remove the cinnamon stick from the salsa rossa and discard it, then season well to taste and spoon it over your lentils. Place 2 sausages, either sliced or whole, on top. Sprinkle with the thyme and serve with a big bowl of steaming broccoli.

pollo alla cacciatora

hunter's chicken stew

Chicken cacciatora seems to be reasonably well known in Britain and the U.S. because it's the classic prepackaged dish you find in Italian food sections in supermarkets (which, to be honest, never taste of much). When you get the real deal cooked at home with love and passion, it's a totally different experience. It's a simple combination of flavors that just works really well. *Cacciatore* means "hunter," so this is obviously the type of food that a hunter's wife cooks for her fella when he gets home from a hard morning spent in the countryside. This is also a great dish for big parties, as it looks after itself in the oven. In the picture I've made it for about twelve people.

1 4½-lb. chicken, cut up, or use the
  equivalent amount of chicken pieces
sea salt and freshly ground black pepper
8 bay leaves
2 sprigs of fresh rosemary
3 cloves of garlic, peeled (1 crushed,
  2 sliced)

½ a bottle of Chianti
flour, for dusting
extra virgin olive oil
6 anchovy fillets
a handful of green or black olives, pitted
2 14-oz. cans of good-quality plum tomatoes

Season the chicken pieces with salt and freshly ground black pepper and put them into a bowl. Add the bay leaves, rosemary sprigs, and the crushed clove of garlic and cover with the wine. Leave to marinate for at least an hour, but preferably overnight in the fridge.

Preheat your oven to 350°F. Drain the chicken, reserving the marinade, and pat dry with paper towels. Dust the chicken pieces with flour and shake off any excess. Heat an ovenproof pan, add a splash of olive oil, fry the chicken pieces until browned lightly all over, and put to one side.

Place the pan back on the heat and add the sliced garlic. Fry gently until golden brown, then add the anchovies, olives, tomatoes (broken up with a wooden spoon), and the chicken pieces with their reserved marinade. Bring to a boil, cover with a lid or a double thickness layer of aluminum foil, and bake in the preheated oven for 1½ hours.

Skim off any oil that's collected on top of the sauce, then stir, taste, and add a little salt and pepper if necessary. Remove the bay leaves and rosemary sprigs and serve with a salad, or some cannellini beans, and plenty of Chianti.

arrosto misto

mixed roast

The concept of arrosto misto is really simple and exciting. As opposed to just roasting a whole chicken or a piece of beef on its own, the idea is that you take all kinds of seasonal meat and game and use any mixture or combo in the same roasting pan – a bit like a grab bag! There is something about having lots of different meats in a pan – it will definitely have your mates thinking you're really accomplished in the kitchen! Feel free to use just one type of meat if you like (I've written the recipe so that you can follow it easily if you choose to do this), but for special occasions do try the whole lot. Each meat can be flavored slightly differently, using herbs or maybe spices. Of course, different meats have different cooking times, so you will be putting them in at different stages, but the finished dish will end up cooked to perfection. In Italy when it comes to roasting they are not interested in pink duck or rare game; instead they will very gently cook the meat all the way through – delicious.

You can guarantee this will be a show-stopping dinner – there's always something festive about a big joint of roast meat, let alone several different ones. And it's great for people to be able to help themselves to a little of what they fancy . . . and then have more! Any leftovers can be made into a lasagne (see page 124).

for the rabbit
14 thin strips of pancetta
olive oil
1 medium-sized rabbit, skinned
sea salt and freshly ground black pepper
4 sprigs of fresh rosemary

for the rabbit stuffing
2 Italian or Cumberland sausages
a handful of breadcrumbs
zest of ½ an orange
a pinch of nutmeg
1 dried red chili, crumbled
a small bunch of fresh sage, leaves picked
    and finely chopped

Preheat your oven to 375°F. Lay the slices of pancetta out on a sheet of oiled waxed paper so they are side by side and slightly overlapping, then place in the fridge.

Rub the rabbit with oil and season with salt and pepper. You now need to make the stuffing, so score the skin of the sausages and remove the meat from the skins. Place the meat in a bowl with the breadcrumbs, orange zest, nutmeg, dried chili, and sage. Season with a little pepper, mix it all together well, and stuff it inside the belly cavity of the rabbit.

Take the pancetta out of the fridge and wrap the waxed paper – pancetta side down – round the belly of the rabbit. Carefully peel the paper off, so the pancetta is left wrapped around the rabbit. Lay the sprigs of rosemary over the pancetta, then tie the rabbit belly in a couple of places, using string to keep the stuffing in place. Place the rabbit in a roasting pan and cook in the preheated oven for an hour. Halfway through, add any extra orange halves, pieces of pancetta, or sprigs of herbs to the pan, then baste the meat and return it to the oven.

(continued on page 227)

for the duck

1 4½-lb. duck
olive oil
sea salt and freshly ground black pepper
a sprig of fresh sage

a stick of cinnamon
3 or 4 cloves of garlic, unpeeled, left whole
½ an orange

Preheat the oven to 375°F. Rub the duck with oil, season with salt and pepper, and stuff it with the sage, cinnamon stick, garlic cloves, and orange half. Place in a roasting pan and cook in the preheated oven for 2 hours. Halfway through, add any extra garlic cloves, orange halves, or sprigs of herbs to the pan, then baste the meat and return it to the oven.

for the chicken

1 4-lb. free-range chicken
olive oil
sea salt and freshly ground black pepper
6 bay leaves

3 cloves of garlic, unpeeled, left whole
1 lemon, halved

Preheat the oven to 375°F. Rub the chicken with oil, season with salt and pepper, and stuff it with the bay leaves, garlic, and lemon halves. Place in a roasting pan and cook in the preheated oven for 1½ hours. Halfway through, add any extra garlic cloves, lemon halves, or herbs you may have to the pan, then baste the meat and return it to the oven.

for the squab and quail

2 11-oz. squab
4 6½-oz. quail
olive oil
sea salt and freshly ground black pepper
a bunch of thyme
a bulb of garlic, cloves unpeeled

6 strips of orange rind
8 strips of lemon rind
8 fresh sage leaves
4 1-inch-square pieces of pancetta or bacon

Preheat the oven to 375°F. Rub the squab and quail with oil, season with salt and pepper, and stuff them with a few sprigs of thyme, the cloves of garlic, and the strips of orange rind. Lay the strips of lemon rind over the quail breasts. Cover each piece of lemon rind with a sage leaf, and cover with a square of pancetta. Secure these onto each quail with string. Place in a roasting pan and cook in the preheated oven for 35 minutes. Halfway through, add any extra garlic, lemon and orange halves, pieces of pancetta, or sprigs of herbs to the pan, then baste the meat and return it to the oven.

To serve

Serve your chosen meat or the whole arrosto misto on a big serving dish with all the juices and garlic from the pan. Roasted veg is perfect served alongside. Give everyone a steak knife, a napkin, a fingerbowl, and plenty of Chianti!

my thoughts on rabbit

If you ask British or American people if they've ever eaten rabbit most of them will wince, without having once tried it. The funny thing is, when it's on the menu at my restaurant it sells out before anything else. Where it is available in supermarkets, most people just walk past it and never buy it. My nan ate rabbit all her life, especially after the war when it was cheap and plentiful, and my mum grew up on it. She remembers seeing rabbits hanging up at the butcher's, all unskinned – you don't normally see this nowadays, which is a real shame. I want to inspire you to have a go at cooking this wonderful healthy meat which tastes a bit like chicken.

You can buy free-range farmed rabbits, which are tender and juicy, or wild ones, which have a lot more flavor. Try to get hold of wild rabbit if you can. Whenever you buy a rabbit, you pretty much always get the whole thing, so ask your butcher to cut it into legs and shoulders, remove the belly, and cut the saddle into four pieces. You'll always get a couple of livers and kidneys, which taste gorgeous, as well. Your butcher should be more than happy to cut your rabbit for you. If you want to have a go at cutting it yourself, don't think you need to be too precise, because I've eaten this in Italy with the rabbit simply chopped up into erratic bits, and it's been beautiful.

coniglio marinato alla griglia

serves 2

grilled and marinated rabbit

I've written this recipe to be cooked on the barbecue, because the flavor will be amazing, but it also works really well when roasted in the oven at 400°F. If you cook it in the oven, turn the pieces of rabbit several times to ensure even color and cooking. If you cook it on the barbecue, you'll need five wooden or metal skewers (soak wooden ones before you use them). Whether barbecuing or roasting, see the picture for your rough timings.

1 2½-lb rabbit, preferably wild, cut up
a handful of fresh thyme and rosemary,
  leaves picked
4 garlic cloves, peeled
olive oil

zest and juice of 1 lemon
1 teaspoon honey
2 sprigs of fresh thyme
salt and freshly ground black pepper
4 thick slices of pancetta

Put your rabbit pieces into a bowl. Using a pestle and mortar, or a blender, bash or whiz up the thyme and rosemary leaves to a pulp, then add the garlic cloves and bash or whiz again. Stir in 8 tablespoons of olive oil, the lemon zest and juice, and the honey, and pour this over the rabbit. Put the meat to one side and let it come to room temperature while you light your barbecue (see page 191).

Now I'm going to talk about flavor. Tie your thyme sprigs together like a little brush. Each time you turn the meat, dab it with a little of the marinade to give you a lovely encrusted layer of flavor. This rabbit is going to be really tasty!

Keeping the marinade to one side, remove the pieces of meat and season with salt and pepper. Sandwich 2 slices of pancetta between the 2 pieces of belly using 3 skewers (see picture). Put the legs and shoulder on the barbecue. When they've been cooking for 10 minutes, put the belly on. After another 10 minutes put the saddle and ribs on. Make sure you turn the meat over every so often. Look after it by controlling the temperature and basting it continuously with the marinade. Cut three-quarters of the way through each kidney and open it out like a book. Cut the liver into 4 pieces and push one piece onto each remaining skewer, followed by a kidney and more liver.

When all the pieces of meat are beautifully cooked, add your skewered bits of kidney and liver onto the barbecue and cook until golden, along with your 2 remaining slices of pancetta. After a few minutes, when the pancetta is browned, put it on top of the meat at the cooler end of the barbie. Now get your guests around the table.

You can serve the rabbit with any white beans, or roast potatoes, or grilled vegetables, or different salads – it really depends on how you feel and what the weather's like. Just put a big bowl of your chosen accompaniment in the middle of the table and serve all the meat on a board. Lovely with a glass of white wine. Simple, honest, and bloody good.

belly: 25 to 30 minutes

kidneys and liver: 4 minutes

saddle and ribs: 15 to 20 minutes

legs and shoulder: 35 to 40 minutes

costolette di maiale con salvia serves 4

pork chops with sage

Pork chops are a pretty regular occurrence in Italy. They can be cooked in many, many ways, but this recipe is one of my favorites. When I first saw it being made in a trattoria in Florence, on my first-ever trip to Italy, the young lady who was making it inserted a small paring knife into the side of the chops and moved it from side to side to create a little pocket inside the meat. It was clever, as you couldn't tell from the outside that this "flavor pocket" was there. A little pork fat or butter can be rubbed inside the pocket and then you can add some prosciutto fat, or smashed-up chestnuts or walnuts (depending on what's in season). A little fresh sage should always be added, and maybe a little garlic. I like to add a tiny amount of lemon zest as well, as it's best friends with pork. Have a go at trying this pocket trick.

2½ lb. all-purpose potatoes, peeled and diced	4 tablespoons butter, finely diced
sea salt and freshly ground black pepper	4 dried apricots
4 thick pork chops, on the bone	extra virgin olive oil
24 fresh sage leaves	flour
1 bulb of garlic	6 thick strips of pancetta or
4 slices of prosciutto	bacon (½ inch thick, if possible), or an 8-oz. package of pancetta lardons

Preheat the oven to 425°F. Put your potatoes into a pot of salted water and bring to a boil. Give them 3 or 4 minutes – you only want to parboil them – then drain them and allow them to steam dry. Lay your pork chops on a board and insert a small paring knife horizontally into the side of each chop to make a hidden pocket. Make sure the tip of your knife stays in the middle of the chop, as you don't want to cut through the meat to either side. Be careful – watch your fingers!

Set aside 8 of the largest sage leaves. Add 8 more leaves to your food processor with a peeled clove of garlic, the prosciutto, butter, apricots, and a pinch of salt and pepper and give it a whiz. This is now a beautifully flavored butter that can be divided between the pork chops and pushed into the pockets.

Dress the 8 large sage leaves that you set aside with a little oil and press one side of them into some flour. Press a leaf, flour side down, onto each side of the chops (so you have 2 leaves on each chop). Leave the chops on a plate, covered with plastic wrap, to come to room temperature while you get your potatoes ready.

If you're using thick strips of pancetta, slice them into matchsticks, as thick as a pencil. Put them into a large roasting pan, with your potatoes, the remaining sage leaves, and the rest of your whole unpeeled garlic cloves. Drizzle with a little extra virgin olive oil and put the pan into the preheated oven. After 10 minutes, put a frying pan on the burner and get it very hot. Add a touch of olive oil and put in your seasoned pork chops. Fry for 10 minutes, until golden and crisp on both sides, then remove the pan of potatoes from the oven – they should be nice and light golden by now – and place the chops on top. Put the pan back into the oven for 10–15 minutes, depending on how thick the chops are, then remove the pan from the oven and serve.

stracotto di fagiano

serves 4–6

pheasant stew

I made this simple stew with the pheasants I got when I went shooting with some gamekeepers in Tuscany. It's a pretty basic stew, with the addition of roasted chestnuts which give a lovely flavor and thickness to the sauce. If, like in London and New York, you come across a street vendor roasting chestnuts, buy a bag. The other alternative is vac-packed chestnuts, but they never taste quite as good as the ones you can buy roasted. When it comes to serving suggestions, this can be eaten as a stew, or the meat can be torn off the bone and served with a pasta such as pappardelle. If you chop it up a bit finer it will go well with rigatoni, or with pici (see page 105).

3 hen pheasants, cut into legs and breasts
sea salt and freshly ground black pepper
6 juniper berries, crushed
3 tablespoons flour
olive oil
1 small red onion, peeled and chopped
1 carrot, peeled and chopped

3 sticks of celery, chopped
4 cloves of garlic, peeled and chopped
2 cups red wine
3 bay leaves
a sprig of fresh rosemary
7 oz. roasted and peeled chestnuts
2 tablespoons mascarpone

Preheat your oven to 400°F. Season the pheasant pieces well with salt and pepper and the crushed juniper berries and dust with the flour. On the stove, heat a saucepan big enough to hold all the ingredients and add a splash of olive oil. Fry the pheasant pieces until golden all over and remove to a plate.

Using the same pan, turn the heat down and add the chopped onion, carrot, celery, and garlic. Cook gently until the vegetables are soft and lightly browned. Add the wine, bay leaves, and rosemary, then place the pheasant pieces back in the pan with the chestnuts. Bring to a boil, cover tightly with a double-thickness piece of aluminum foil or a lid, and bake in the preheated oven for around 2 hours.

Remove the pheasant pieces from the pan with a pair of tongs and keep them warm. Skim any fat off the surface of the stewing liquor, remove the rosemary twig and bay leaves, stir in the mascarpone, and simmer so it reduces slightly. Put the meat back into the pan, warm through, and serve with polenta.

schiacciata di manzo con aglio, rosmarino, e funghi

serves 4 as a starter, 2 as a main

flash roast beef with garlic, rosemary, and mushrooms

Schiacciata is the sister dish of carpaccio, but while carpaccio's raw, this is literally flashed in the oven so it just turns color. Obviously the better the beef the better the dish. So go for something with good marbling and a bit of integrity. It can also be served as a starter or a snack, with different salads sprinkled on top. The truffle oil's optional, but the flavor is interesting, so give it a try because it's something new. This whole dish is impressive and damn tasty.

1¼ lb. good-quality beef fillet, sinews
  removed, cut into ½-inch slices
extra virgin olive oil
optional: a few drops of truffle oil
2 sprigs of fresh rosemary, leaves picked
1 clove of garlic, peeled and finely sliced
3 handfuls of arugula
a large handful of mixed salad leaves
  including radicchio di Treviso or
  salad radicchio

a handful of really firm mushrooms,
  such as chanterelles, field, or
  uovoli (Caesar) mushrooms
balsamic vinegar
sea salt and freshly ground black pepper
a block of Parmesan cheese

OK, first things first – whack your oven onto its highest heat. For this dish we're going to cook the meat on the platter it will be served on, so ideally use one of those classic cheap old metal pans or trays. Or you can use regular serving plates instead, if you know they're heatproof. Rub them with extra virgin olive oil or truffle oil. And now you're going to prepare the meat. Work with one piece at a time, and put it on a 12-inch piece of garbage bag with another piece on top. Using a rolling pin, evenly slap the meat until it's four times the width you started with, but a quarter of the thickness.

Lay the meat on your tray, platter, or plate right to the edges – you can let it hang over a tiny bit. Put your rosemary leaves into a sieve and run hot water over them to get the oils and flavors going. Put them into a little bowl, pour 3 or 4 tablespoons of extra virgin olive oil on top, and massage the leaves with your fingers to get more flavor out of them. Stir the garlic into the rosemary oil, then pat everything evenly all over the meat. The meat can be prepared to this point a few hours in advance, then wrapped in plastic wrap and kept in the fridge.

Now all you've got to do is get a little salad together. Tear your arugula and radicchio into a large bowl. Slice your mushrooms as thinly as possible and add them to the bowl.

This dish is best put together really quickly at the last minute. All you need to do is put the meat in the preheated oven for 1–3 minutes (depending on your oven). By the time you've dressed the salad, with a little extra virgin olive oil, balsamic vinegar, salt, and pepper, and put your block of Parmesan on the table with a speed peeler for shaving pieces off it, you can take the meat out of the oven – it should be paler in color now. The idea is not to cook the meat, but simply to warm it through. Scatter the salad over the meat and serve it straight away. Shave over some Parmesan and have a nice glass of wine with it. Tasty, tasty, and very gorgeous!

spiedini di involtini di agnello e funghi

serves 4

lamb and mushroom kebabs

In Italy there are many different versions of rolled and stuffed meat, fish, and vegetables, skewered either on metal skewers or on sprigs of rosemary. Of course, this is tasty and colorful cooking – and to roast or barbecue these things is always exciting – but traditionally this type of food was considered poor people's cooking. They would skewer different combinations of vegetables and herbs to make them look like rich people's game-bird kebabs. In peasant cooking they would try to stretch their meat a little further by bulking it out with veg, as this was much cheaper.

The general idea for this recipe is to get a slice of meat (from a leg of lamb or a cutlet, or you can use pork or chicken) and bash it out between two pieces of plastic wrap using something heavy and flat. This makes the meat bigger and thinner and tenderizes it as well. You can make life super-easy by asking your butcher to get the meat ready for you. Tell him you're going to be making rolled and skewered lamb and that you need about 1½ lb., sliced into twelve pieces and batted out flat, about a quarter inch thick. (For the price of a phone call you can save fifteen minutes of banging in the kitchen!) You can then stuff, roll, or fold the meat and skewer it. I skewered mine with bay sticks. The combination I'm giving you here is really earthy and full of mountain flavors like mushrooms and oregano, or marjoram – really simple and delicious. If you're lucky enough to get hold of fresh porcini, fantastic – if not, any firm mushroom will be fine.

olive oil
1½ lb. lamb, batted into 12 thin pieces
a large handful of fresh oregano or
  marjoram, leaves picked
1 clove of garlic, peeled
8 anchovy fillets

zest and juice of 1 lemon
salt and freshly ground black pepper
4 rosemary or bay sticks, or
  4 wooden skewers
8 medium-sized porcini, cèpes, or field
  mushrooms, halved or quartered

Rub a clean kitchen surface with a little olive oil and lay your pieces of meat out next to each other in a line. In a pestle and mortar, bash up your oregano or marjoram. Add your garlic and anchovy fillets and bash to a paste. Add the lemon juice and twice as much olive oil. Mix up and taste – it should be quite lemony but it will mellow when cooked. Season, then smear and rub this flavored oil evenly over your pieces of meat and sprinkle a little lemon zest over the top.

Preheat the oven to 400°F. Now make your *involtini*. Roll each piece of meat up so that the rolls are about half the size of a cigar but a little thicker. If you're going to use bay or rosemary sticks, peel off the leaves to the length you want and sharpen the tips. (Reserve any bay leaves as you can add these to your kebabs.) Skewer a piece of rolled meat first, followed by a piece of mushroom, and then a bay leaf (if using). Continue until you have three bits of each on each skewer. Place on a baking sheet and drizzle with olive oil. Roast in the preheated oven for 7 minutes, or cook on a barbecue for about 3½ minutes each side. Serve drizzled with olive oil, as part of a mixed grill or with a nice salad, some bread, and a wedge of lemon.

cosciotto d'agnello ripieno di olive, pane, pinoli, e erbe aromatiche

serves 6

leg of lamb stuffed with olives, bread, pinenuts, and herbs

Roasting a leg of lamb is still one of the most nostalgic times for me. A thousand pictures go through my head just thinking about my old man slicing lamb on a Sunday. This brilliant roast lamb dish uses Italian staples to make a delicious stuffing – it's nice to get all the herbs in the ingredients list, but if you can only get hold of a couple, don't worry.

Try to buy the lamb from your own butcher or a supermarket with a qualified butcher's section. Tell them you want a nice leg of lamb, preferably organic, with the H-bone and thighbone tunnel-boned and removed. This sounds complicated but it's just butchers' jargon. It means the top half of the leg has the bone removed, leaving just the ankle bone, allowing you to stuff it. For the veg, turnips, Jerusalem artichokes, celeriac, fennel, and parsnips are all good.

1 whole bulb of garlic, broken into
  cloves, unpeeled
3 good handfuls of mixed fresh
  herbs (mint, parsley, oregano, thyme),
  leaves picked
6 slices of pancetta
3 anchovy fillets
3½–4 oz. rustic bread, torn into
  1-inch pieces (don't use prepackaged
  sliced bread)
a large handful of pinenuts

a handful of green olives, pits removed
sea salt and freshly ground black pepper
1 4½-lb. leg of lamb, prepped as above
a large bunch of fresh rosemary
olive oil
4½ lb. good roasting spuds, peeled
  and halved
a sprig of bay leaves
a bottle of red wine

Peel a couple of garlic cloves and pop them into a food processor – as it's whizzing, add your mixed herbs. Add the pancetta and anchovies and whiz again. Scrape the mixture into a bowl and add the bread to the processor. Whiz to coarse breadcrumbs, and add to the bowl with the pinenuts and olives. Add salt and pepper and scrunch everything together with your hands. If it looks too dry, add a drop of boiling water. Push the stuffing into the cavity in the lamb. You can roast it stuffed like this, or you can tie it up with string, pushing some rosemary underneath. Pat it with olive oil on the outside and season with salt and pepper.

Toss the potatoes and remaining garlic with the bay leaves, the rest of the rosemary, some olive oil, and salt and pepper and put them into a roasting pan with the lamb in the middle. It's unusual to see rare or pink roasted meats in Italy, so we're going to cook our lamb like they do. Roast it for about an hour and a half at 400°F. Trust me – it will be juicy and delicious! After half an hour, the Italian way is to start basting the lamb with a swig of wine over the meat and veg every 15 minutes or so until the meat is cooked. Remove the potatoes to a dish when cooked, to keep them warm.

When the lamb is cooked, let it rest for 15 minutes. It's nice served with some simply cooked greens. The Italians prefer that the goodness from the meat juices be cooked into the vegetables in the pan rather than make gravy.

sugo di cinghiale di mercatello

serves 6–8

wild boar sauce from mercatello

This young girl was really excited when her dad was preparing the wild boar which he had caught. She knew that the animal had to be cleaned, skinned, and gutted before it could be cooked, but what shocked me was how normal it was for all the kids who were playing nearby. Can you imagine if this was happening in Britain or the U.S.? And as for the use of the paddling pool . . . !

I know that wild boar is a little difficult to get hold of unless you have a great butcher or farmers' market nearby, but venison, pork, beef, or lamb cooked this way will also be absolutely delicious. A shoulder cut will work best. If the meat's cut into pieces about 1 inch square, the finished meat sauce can be served as a stew on its own, with some bread or on polenta (see page 269), and if it's cut into ½-inch dice it can be mixed with pappardelle. If you slice the meat even smaller, or mince it up, it will be fantastic with tagliatelle.

2¼ lb. shoulder of wild boar or venison, trimmed of fat and sinews
2 large carrots, peeled
2 onions, peeled
6 sticks of celery
a handful of fresh sage, leaves picked
1 teaspoon juniper berries

sea salt and freshly ground black pepper
1 bottle of white wine
4 strips of pancetta or bacon, finely sliced
2–3 small dried chilies, to taste
olive oil
1 1½-lb. jar of passata
optional: a handful of freshly grated Parmesan cheese

Decide how you want to serve your sauce and cut your meat into the appropriate size dice (see above). Put it into a bowl. Take half your carrots, onions, and celery and roughly chop them. Add them to the meat. Bash up the sage with the juniper berries in a pestle and mortar and toss with the meat and vegetables. Season with pepper and add half the white wine, topping up with a little water. Leave the meat to marinate overnight.

The next day, fry the pancetta and chili in a pan with a little olive oil, until lightly golden and crisp. Chop the remaining carrot, celery, and onion, add to the pan, and cook slowly on a medium heat for 10 to 15 minutes, until the vegetables have softened. Meanwhile, remove the meat from its marinade, discarding the liquid and vegetables. Turn the heat right up and add the meat to the pan. Cook until nearly all its natural liquid has evaporated – this takes some time but will help to intensify the flavors – then add the rest of the white wine. Stir together and continue cooking until the liquid has nearly gone, then add the sauce and a little water. Season well with salt and pepper, turn the heat down, and simmer for around 1½–2½ hours (depending on the size of your pieces of meat), until lovely and tender, adding a little more water if the sauce gets too thick. Correct the seasoning before serving.

If serving with pasta, cook it in salted boiling water according to the package instructions and drain it, reserving a little of the cooking water. Toss the pasta with the sauce, adding a little Parmesan and some of the cooking water to loosen if necessary. Divide among your plates and sprinkle over a little more Parmesan.

contorni *side dishes*

side dishes

In Italy, the way they break their menus down means that by the time you reach your *secondo* you will literally get just a piece of meat or fish on your plate with a little juice or oil drizzled over the top. Very simple and very delicious, but made even better when served with a *contorno*, or side dish. These can be enjoyed in their own right, similar to antipasti – some simply cooked greens, beans, or potatoes, for instance. This chapter's meant to give you a little inspiration for things to serve alongside your meat or fish. Generally, when *contorni* are served in Italy you'll have little bowls or plates in the middle of the table to help yourself from. The main emphasis when it comes to cooking the vegetables is to do it simply.

About 75 percent of Italian fruit and veg comes from Puglia in the southeast (on the "heel" of the country). This region is considered the garden of Italy – it's flat or gently undulating countryside and much easier to farm. However, in hillier parts of the country, where the landscape might sometimes be quite extreme, you'll often see vegetables being farmed up the side of a hill, to be picked and sold locally.

Beans are a big thing in Italy. Everyone loves them there! They're cooked freshly shelled and take hardly any time at all. I've given you a recipe for Italian style beans on page 256 which shows you the best way to cook any of the different types, fresh or dried. Cranberry and cannellini beans are usually dried for the winter months, to be used in soups or as side dishes, and take longer to cook than fresh, but if they're dried properly and if they're from the previous season they can be absolutely delicious.

Polenta is another Italian staple. It can be cooked wet or firm (see page 269), and is served up alongside meat and fish in much the same way that we might serve potatoes in Britain or the States. If you've never tried it, do give it a go.

vignole

serves 4

spring vegetable stew

Vignole, or vignarola, is a Roman word to describe this incredible stew which is a celebration of spring. Please, please try it – you will end up making it forever! If you don't have any chicken stock on hand, just use some of the water you cooked the beans, leeks, and chard in. You can leave the cooked prosciutto in or take it out before serving, as you like. This is absolutely lovely tossed into cooked, drained pasta. And you must try it with asparagus if you can.

4 small or violet artichokes
sea salt and freshly ground black pepper
12 oz. shelled fresh baby fava beans
6 baby leeks, or 1 regular leek, outer
  leaves removed, cut into 3-inch lengths,
  washed
½ lb. spinach or chard, picked
  and washed
extra virgin olive oil

1 small white onion, peeled and
  finely chopped
1½ cups chicken stock
12 oz. shelled fresh peas
4 thick slices of prosciutto
a small bunch of fresh mint, leaves
  picked
a small bunch of fresh flat-leaf parsley,
  leaves picked

Put the artichokes into a pot of cold salted water and bring to a boil. Cook for about 10 minutes or until tender (check by inserting a knife into the heart) and drain. Allow to cool, then peel back the outer leaves till you reach the pale tender ones, and remove the choke using a teaspoon. Tear the hearts into quarters.

Fill the pot with water again, add some salt, and bring to a boil. Blanch the fava beans for a minute, then remove from the water with a slotted spoon and drain. Blanch the leeks for 3 or 4 minutes, until tender, and the spinach or chard until just wilted.

Heat a large saucepan, big enough to hold all the ingredients, and add a good splash of oil. Cook the onion very gently for about 10 minutes, until soft, add the chicken stock and the peas, and bring to a boil. Lay the slices of prosciutto over the top and simmer gently for about 10 minutes, until the peas are cooked and soft and the prosciutto has flavored them nicely.

Tear the leeks into strips and stir them into the peas with the roughly chopped spinach or chard, the artichokes, and the fava beans. Bring back to simmering point and let all the vegetables stew together very slowly for about 10 more minutes. Chop the herbs.

Taste, season with salt and pepper, and stir in the chopped herbs and a good few glugs of extra virgin olive oil before serving.

funghi al cartoccio al forno

serves 4

baked mushrooms in a bag

This is a fantastically quick recipe to make, and when you open the bags you'll be rewarded by the most amazing smells from the earthy mushrooms and the herbs. Really nice. Have some string on hand to tie up the herb bundles. PS, You can make this for a family dinner by using one large bag instead of four small ones.

a few sprigs each of fresh bay, sage,
  rosemary, and thyme
4 slices of prosciutto
14 oz. firm wild mushrooms, brushed
  and trimmed

sea salt and freshly ground black pepper
extra virgin olive oil
1 egg, preferably organic, lightly beaten
¾ cup vermouth or white wine

Preheat your oven to 400°F and place a baking sheet on the middle shelf.

To give the mushrooms great flavor, I like to make a herb bundle to go in the bag with them, so make four small bundles using a little bay, sage, rosemary, and thyme in each, tied up with string. To make your bags, get four large sheets of waxed paper about 15 inches square. Lay a piece of prosciutto to one side (just off the center) of each piece of paper and top it with one of your herb bundles and a pile of mushrooms. Season with salt and pepper and drizzle with olive oil. Brush the edges of the paper with the beaten egg, then fold the waxed paper over the mushrooms to create a kind of envelope. Fold the edges over two or three times and scrunch together to keep them in place, but before you fold the last edge, pour a few tablespoons of vermouth or white wine into each parcel.

Making sure the parcels are tightly folded and sealed, place them side by side on the hot baking sheet, and cook in the preheated oven for 15 minutes, until puffed up.

Serve the mushrooms still in their bags so that people can pop their own and smell all the lovely flavors inside. Remember not to eat the herb bundle – it's just there for flavor! This dish can be served alongside meat or fish, or on its own as a snack or antipasti.

radicchio di treviso marinato alla griglia con aglio e aceto balsamico

serves 6

grilled and marinated radicchio di treviso with garlic and balsamic vinegar

This is one of the real tastes of Italy that you must try. Treviso is the Aston Martin of the radicchio family. It gives great results and is especially good when eaten warm like this. Have a go at growing your own – you can buy seeds online from www.seedsofitaly.com and www.growitalian.com.

2 heads of radicchio di Treviso
 (or salad radicchio)
sea salt and freshly ground black pepper
2 cloves of garlic, peeled and chopped
good-quality balsamic vinegar

extra virgin olive oil
3 sprigs of fresh rosemary, leaves picked
 and finely chopped
a small handful of fresh flat-leaf parsley,
 leaves picked

Separate the leaves of the radicchio, wash them, and put them to one side. Add a good pinch of salt to your chopped garlic and, using the side of your knife, squash it into a pulp. Put the mashed garlic into a serving bowl and add a couple of tablespoons of balsamic vinegar. Pour twice as much oil as vinegar over the top and season with salt and pepper. Add the chopped rosemary.

Preheat a griddle pan and grill the radicchio leaves a few at a time for 10 seconds or so, just until they wilt and start to char. Immediately drop them into the dressing and stir them around to coat them with all the lovely flavors. Tear the parsley over it and eat straight away.

fagioli all'italiana

italian style beans

serves 4

Obviously the Italians are big fans of beans, but I don't mean the canned variety in tomato sauce. No, in Italy lots of different types of beans are used as little side dishes, which tend to become the heroes of the meal. They really enhance most meat dishes. The method for cooking beans is generally the same, no matter whether you're doing cannellini, lima, cranberry, or zolfini. The only thing that will differ is the cooking time for each type of bean, and this will depend on whether you're using fresh (you may have to search them out at farmers' markets) or dried.

Fresh will generally take 25 minutes to half an hour, and these would be my preferred choice. However, dried beans can be excellent. The only thing is that they have to be rehydrated in water overnight. During this time the beans will slowly soak up the water, almost to the point where they're like fresh beans again. Whether you're using dried and soaked beans or cooking them fresh, the most effective cooking method I've seen in Italy is the one below.

1 lb. 2 oz. dried or 2 lb. 3 oz. shelled fresh
  beans (cranberry, cannellini, lima, or
  zolfini)
1 potato, peeled
2 ripe tomatoes, squashed
½ a bulb of garlic

a bunch of fresh herbs, tied together with
  string (use rosemary, bay, sage, and thyme)
extra virgin olive oil
herb vinegar
sea salt and freshly ground black pepper

If using dried beans, soak them overnight in clean cold water, then drain and rinse before cooking. Place your beans, dried or fresh, in a deep pot. Cover with cold water but don't add salt (it makes the skins go tough). Add your potato, the squashed tomatoes (these will help to soften the skin), the garlic, the bunch of herbs, and a drizzle of extra virgin olive oil. Place on the heat and bring to a boil. Skim any froth from the surface of the liquid and simmer gently for 40 minutes or until the beans are soft and tender – check them after 25 minutes if using fresh.

Drain the beans of all but about half a glass of their cooking water, and remove and discard the potato, tomatoes, garlic, and herbs. Use the reserved cooking water to dress the beans, then loosen with a good amount of extra virgin olive oil and enough herb vinegar to give a little twang. Season with salt and pepper. The beans can be served as a lovely little side dish, or they can be added to pastas, stews, soups, you name it!

zucchini in padella

serves 4

fried zucchini

This is great as a side dish to go with white meats or fish, as part of an antipasti selection, smeared on crostini, or smashed up and tossed with a little cream, Parmesan, and penne pasta. Also really good in omelettes or frittatas.

3 firm medium zucchini
extra virgin olive oil
3 cloves of garlic, peeled and finely sliced
½ a fresh red chili, sliced, or 1 small dried
  red chili, crumbled
a handful of fresh marjoram or oregano,
  leaves picked, or 1 teaspoon dried
  oregano

sea salt and freshly ground black pepper
3 good-quality anchovy fillets, in olive oil
zest and juice of ½ a lemon
optional: a sprig of fresh mint, leaves picked
  and chopped

First of all, remove the ends from the zucchini and slice them into ½-inch pieces. Feel free to halve them if your zucchini are on the large side.

Put a couple of glugs of olive oil in a pan on a medium heat. Add the sliced garlic and your chili. After 30 seconds, add your zucchini and herbs and season lightly with salt and pepper. Make sure the pan's not too hot – you don't want the zucchini to cook too fast. Give everything a good mix around, then put a lid on so it's slightly ajar and will hold some steam in. Give the pan a little shake or stir every couple of minutes for the next 10 to 12 minutes or so. For the last 2 minutes of cooking, add the anchovy fillets and lemon zest. Once the anchovies have melted, season carefully to taste, adding a squeeze of lemon juice to balance the chili and seasoning. Serve right away – lovely sprinkled with chopped mint.

zucca al forno

roasted squash

Over the years I've seen roasted squash cooked in many ways and I've got to say this particular way is one of my favorites. Even though it's very Tuscan in style, the flavors remind me of English chutney recipes that I've come across in old cookbooks. When roasted like this, the squash is wonderful eaten as part of an antipasti plate, or in soups, or tossed with pasta, or with meat. Other types of squash that are great for roasting are Hubbarb (which has green or orange skin) and acorn squash (which has an orangey-green skin and is a bit more squashed than round). Ask your local fruit and veg man for guidance if you're not sure.

1 large ambercup squash
1 dried red chili
sea salt and freshly ground black pepper

a large handful of fresh sage leaves
1 stick of cinnamon, broken into pieces
olive oil

Preheat your oven to 350°F. Halve the ambercup squash, remove and reserve the seeds, then cut the squash into slices or chunks with the skin left on. Using a pestle and mortar, or a metal bowl with a rolling pin, bash up the dried red chili with a good pinch of salt. Add the whole sage leaves, the pieces of cinnamon, and enough olive oil to loosen the mixture, and rub the whole lot over all the squash pieces so they are well covered.

Place the squash in one layer in a roasting pan and season lightly with salt and pepper. Sprinkle the seeds over, cover tightly with aluminum foil, and bake for 30 minutes, or until the skin of the squash is soft, then remove the foil and cook for another 10 minutes, until the squash is golden and crisp. Remove the cinnamon and tuck in!

ricetta tipica per verdure verdi

italian style greens

This dish can be eaten either cold as an antipasto or warm as a vegetable contorno. The great thing about it is that you can use any combination of greens, such as baby cabbage leaves, Swiss chard, and even salad leaves like butter, Boston, or Romaine. You can easily buy a big bag of spinach, arugula, and watercress and use some yellow celery leaves and other herbs like basil, parsley, sorrel, and fennel tops to give you a good mixture. Most Italians have a vegetable garden, and no matter how big or small it is, they always have greens and veggies on hand. This recipe sees the more robust leaves blanched first, then wilted down in a pan with the salad leaves, herbs, and garlic, until soft and tender.

6 big handfuls of mixed greens, leaves,
    and herbs (see above)
olive oil
2 cloves of garlic, peeled and sliced

sea salt and freshly ground black pepper
good-quality extra virgin olive oil
juice of 1 lemon

Blanch the more robust leaves like cabbage and chard to perfection in a pot of salted boiling water for a couple of minutes, then drain in a colander and leave to cool down a little. Put a couple of good glugs of olive oil into a large frying pan or casserole type dish and add the sliced garlic. As soon as it starts to take on the smallest amount of color, throw in your salad leaves, then the cabbage and chard. Cook on a medium heat for about 4–5 minutes, moving the greens around the pan with a spoon or a pair of tongs, then add your herbs and cook for a further minute. Remove from the heat and season carefully to taste with salt and pepper, some good-quality extra virgin olive oil, and enough lemon juice to give it a little kick.

melanzane alla parmigiana

serves 6

eggplant parmigiana

This classic northern Italian recipe is a great way to serve eggplant. By layering the eggplant with Parmesan and tomatoes and then baking them, you get an absolutely scrumptious vegetable dish. Great served with all sorts of roasted meats and with roasted fish as well. One of the tweaks I really like doing with this recipe is to grill the eggplant – this makes it a bit more creamy on the inside – instead of frying it in oil, which tends to make it greasy.

3 large firm eggplants
olive oil
1 onion, peeled and finely chopped
½ a bulb of spring garlic, if you can get it, or 1 clove of regular garlic, peeled and finely sliced
1 heaping teaspoon dried oregano
2 14-oz. cans of good-quality plum tomatoes or 2¼ lb. fresh ripe tomatoes

sea salt and freshly ground black pepper
a little wine vinegar
a large handful of fresh basil leaves
4 large handfuls of freshly grated Parmesan cheese
2 handfuls of dried breadcrumbs
a little fresh oregano, leaves chopped
optional: 1 5-oz. ball of buffalo mozzarella

First things first: remove the stems from the eggplants, slice them up into ½-inch-thick slices, and put to one side. Whether you're using a griddle pan or a barbecue, get it really hot. Meanwhile, put 2 or 3 glugs of olive oil into a large pan on a medium heat. Add the onion, garlic, and dried oregano and cook for 10 minutes, until the onion is soft and the garlic has a tiny bit of color. If you're using canned tomatoes, break them up, and if you're using fresh tomatoes (which will obviously taste sweeter and more delicious, if they're in season), very quickly prick each one and put them into a big pan of boiling water for 40 seconds. Remove from the pan with a slotted spoon and put them into a bowl of cold water for 30 seconds, then remove the skins, carefully squeeze out the seeds, and cut up the flesh. Add the tomato flesh or canned tomatoes to the onion, garlic, and oregano. Give the mixture a good stir, then put a lid on the pan and simmer slowly for 15 minutes.

Meanwhile, grill the eggplants on both sides until lightly charred – you may have to do them in batches, as they probably won't all fit into your griddle pan in one go. As each batch is finished, remove them to a tray and carry on grilling the rest, until they're all nicely done. When the tomato sauce is reduced and sweet, season it carefully with salt, pepper, and a tiny swig of wine vinegar, and add the basil. You can leave the sauce chunky or you can purée it.

Get yourself an earthenware type dish (10 x 5–6 inches). Put in a small layer of tomato sauce, then a thin scattering of Parmesan, followed by a single layer of eggplant. Repeat these layers until you've used all the ingredients up, finishing with a little sauce and another good sprinkling of Parmesan. I like to toss the bread crumbs in olive oil with a little freshly chopped oregano and sprinkle them on top of the Parmesan. Sometimes the dish is served with torn-up mozzarella on top, which is nice too. Place the dish in the oven and bake at 375°F for half an hour, until golden, crisp, and bubbly. It's best eaten straight away, but it can also be served cold. You can use the same method substituting zucchini or fennel for the eggplants – both are delicious. But do try making it with eggplants – you'll love it!

polenta

Polenta is cooked ground cornmeal and is a fantastic thing to eat. It's always a good idea to get hold of new season's polenta if you can because it will have more flavor. There are two types – yellow and white – and both are delicious. White polenta comes from around Venice, has a subtler flavor, and tends to be used with fish dishes. Polenta is traditionally grown and harvested in northern Italy, but it's eaten across the country. Each region has its own unique way of serving it. It's boiled in a similar way to porridge, and can be enriched with butter and Parmesan and eaten "wet" as a base for stews or rich sauces. It can also be served firm or with roasted and stewed meats.

If you're at home cooking polenta for friends and you don't want to be running around when they arrive, you can cook it in advance. When it's reached the right consistency, pour it into a bowl, season it, drizzle it with oil, and cover it with waxed paper. Sit it above a pan filled with simmering water on a low heat and that will just keep it warm. When you need to use it, whip off the paper and serve away.

firm polenta

8-9oz new season's polenta   about 3 pints water

Bring a large pan of salted water to a boil and slowly whisk in the polenta. As soon as it starts to boil it will start blipping all over the place, so put a lid on the pan, slightly ajar, so you don't get hot polenta spitting at you, and turn the heat right down. When it thickens up a little it won't be quite so aggressive. When I was a trainee chef I used to walk fast past the polenta pan in case it spat at me! Try to give it a stir every 4 or 5 minutes, getting right into the sides of the pan. It will be getting thick but don't worry. Cook for about 40 to 45 minutes – you're looking for the consistency of fluffy mashed potato.

Correct the seasoning with salt and pepper, then rub a baking sheet or work surface with a little oil and turn the polenta out onto it. Using a palette knife or spoon, move it around until it's about 1 inch thick – don't worry about being neat and tidy when you do this, as it doesn't have to be exact. When the polenta is cooked you'll get a thin crust like a tortilla stuck to the bottom of the pan and I think this is the best bit – a prize for the chef! Chisel this crust off the pan with a palette knife and break it into little crisps. Put these on a plate, sprinkle them with Parmesan and some chopped fresh chilli, drizzle with good olive oil and check out how tasty it is! After half an hour the polenta will have cooled down and you'll be able to cut it into squares, cubes, or slices depending on how you want to grill or pan-fry it.

wet polenta

Use exactly the same measurements as above. After about half an hour's cooking, add a little more water so the consistency's like thickly whipped cream, i.e. slightly looser. It should thickly but easily lollop off the end of a spoon. Once it's cooked, remove the pan from the heat and add 7 tablespoons of butter and 4½ oz. of freshly grated Parmesan. Mix together and carefully season to taste. This wet polenta is then ready to be served.

dolci *desserts*

Roma

VIA VINCENZO BRUNACCI, 33   00146 ROMA TEL. 06/5565745

desserts

This is an interesting one. I don't normally make desserts these days unless it's for a special occasion or on the weekend with the kids. If it's a normal day and we feel like having a dessert, I'll do something really simple.

I was quite surprised to find that most people in Italy don't make desserts either. Instead, they'll buy them from a good shop, either a *gelateria* or a *pasticceria,* where they will have been freshly made that day. They don't see the point of cluttering up their kitchens trying to make things that can be bought much more easily locally from someone who makes them well. Sometimes if Italians are asked to someone's house for dinner they'll take a dessert, the way we might take along a bottle of wine. In general, Italians aren't as fancy with their desserts as the French are, but when they make things like their rustic tortes, or delicious ice creams and sorbets, they're pretty hard to match.

This chapter is full of really simple desserts, from sticky figs eaten with some pecorino cheese to the easiest blackberry tart (so, so simple and ideal for a summer's day) to a tangy lemon sherbet. And, of course, the classic tiramisu.

uva fragola surgelata con cioccolato
e grappa
frozen fragola grapes with chocolate and grappa

My mate Mr. David Loftus (the food photographer I've used for all but the first of my books) obviously loves food as he spends half his life taking pictures of it. When we were in Italy shooting the pictures for the book, he said I should freeze my grapes – which immediately made me think he was a raving heathen! God knows what my friends the grape-pickers would have said. Why on earth would you get beautiful fresh grapes and then freeze them?

But . . . of course, it was a fantastic idea and I was completely wrong!

When David brought the frozen grapes outside for us to eat, it was an incredibly hot and sweltering day, and they were just what we needed to cool us down. He'd managed to get hold of some nice sweet fragola grapes, which are a joy to eat but quite rare in supermarkets. A good muscat grape or any other grape variety that you enjoy eating would also work well. As soon as the grapes start to freeze, all the flesh and juice inside turns into a sort of ice pop–type sorbet, and the outside remains firm (and beautifully frosted).

The best way to eat frozen grapes is with a few bits of good-quality chocolate after a meal, and a nice glass of grappa. If, like me, you are a bit skeptical about this dessert, please try it – it's super cool. Well done, Dave!

sorbetto di pere

pear sorbet

Sorbets are always a nice way to finish a meal if you don't want anything too heavy. They can also be used as palate cleansers between courses. Either way, a sorbet is pretty much always made the same way – a fruit purée is mixed with a little sugar syrup in the right quantity to make it freeze. It will become really shiny and soft to scoop.

This particular recipe for pear and grappa sorbet is a wicked combo and one of my favorites, so give it a go. It's great served in a bowl with lovely soft fruits scattered over the top. A good-quality vodka instead of grappa would be quite interesting, and without wanting to sound like a nutcase, absinthe would be nice too, but to be honest most good supermarkets and liquor stores sell grappa these days. Nardini is a particularly good brand.

This recipe will make enough for six people to have a couple of scoops each, but for four you can make this amount and keep the rest in the freezer for another day. I suggest you use a fairly shallow earthenware or thick porcelain dish that you can put in the freezer beforehand – this speeds up the freezing process for the sorbet.

Try to get really ripe pears – even the ones they sell cheaply in the market. If they're really really ripe and soft to the touch, simply remove the skin and put the flesh into a bowl – you won't need to cook them at all. This is how I did it in Italy when the fruit guy called Pippo at the weekly Terranuova Bracciolini market near Montevarchi gave me a whole tray of pears for free. Go and say hello and he might do the same for you!

¾ cup sugar	juice and zest of 1 lemon
1 cup water	¼ cup grappa, or to taste
2½ lb. soft pears, peeled, quartered, and cores removed	

First of all, put the sugar and water into a pan on the stovetop. Bring to a boil, then reduce the heat and simmer for 3 minutes. Add your quartered pears and, unless they're super soft, continue to simmer for 5 minutes. Remove from the heat, leave to one side for 5 minutes, then add the lemon juice (minus the seeds) and zest. Pour everything into a food processor and whiz to a purée, then push the mixture through a coarse sieve into the dish in which you want to serve it.

Add the grappa, give it a good stir, and taste. The grappa shouldn't be overbearing or too powerful – it should be subtle and should work well with the pears. However, different brands do vary in strength and flavor, so add to taste. (This isn't an excuse to add the whole bottle, though, because if you use too much alcohol the sorbet won't freeze.) Put the dish into the freezer and whisk it up with a fork every half hour – you'll see it becoming pale in color. After a couple of hours it will be ready. The texture should be nice and scoopable. Delicious served with *ventagli* or other delicate crunchy biscuits.

PS, This sorbet will last in the freezer for a couple of days – after that it will crystallize.

crostata di fichi

fig tart

This fantastic tart is one of the things that really sums up Tuscan desserts for me. It's a great way to use ripe figs or stone fruit, with a dusting of cinnamon to bring out the flavor.

15 whole figs, washed
2 tablespoons sugar
2 tablespoons water
2 sprigs of fresh thyme, leaves picked
zest of 1 orange

for the shortcrust pastry
9 tablespoons unsalted butter
1 cup powdered sugar
a small pinch of salt
2 cups all-purpose flour
optional: 1 vanilla bean, scored
  lengthwise and seeds removed
zest of ½ a lemon

2 large egg yolks, preferably organic
2 tablespoons cold milk or water

for the frangipane
10 oz. blanched whole almonds
6 tablespoons all-purpose flour
1 cup plus 2 tablespoons unsalted butter
14 tablespoons sugar
2 large eggs, preferably organic, lightly
  beaten
1 vanilla bean, scored lengthwise and
  seeds removed
1 tablespoon grappa

First, using a little of your butter, you will need to grease an 11-inch tart tin with a removable bottom. To make your pastry, cream together the butter, powdered sugar, and salt and rub in the flour, vanilla seeds, lemon zest, and egg yolks – you can do all this by hand or in a food processor. When the mixture looks like coarse breadcrumbs, add the cold milk or water. Pat and gently work the mixture together until you have a ball of dough, then flour it lightly. Don't work the pastry too much, otherwise it will become elastic and chewy, not flaky and short as you want it to be. Wrap the dough in plastic wrap and place in the fridge for at least an hour. Remove it from the fridge, roll it out, and line your tart tin. Place in the freezer for an hour.

Preheat the oven to 350°F and bake the pastry case for around 12 minutes or until lightly golden. Remove from the oven and turn the heat down to 325°F.

To make the frangipane, blitz 9 oz. of the whole almonds in a food processor until you have a fine powder, and transfer this to a bowl with the flour. Now blitz the butter and sugar until light and creamy. Add this to the almonds with the lightly beaten eggs, the vanilla seeds, and the grappa and fold in until completely mixed and smooth. Place in the fridge for at least half an hour to firm up. Remove the stems from the figs, score each one on the top in the shape of a cross, then using your thumb push up from the base to open it out.

Spoon the chilled frangipane mixture into the pastry case, then lightly push the figs into the frangipane with the scored side up. Heat the sugar with the water and drizzle this syrup over the figs. Roughly chop the remaining almonds and sprinkle over the top with the thyme leaves and orange zest. Bake in the preheated oven for about 40 minutes, or until the frangipane mixture has become firm and golden on the outside but is still soft in the middle. Allow to cool for about 30 to 40 minutes. Lovely served with a dollop of mascarpone or crème fraîche.

bustrengo

bolognese polenta and apple cake

This is a superb moist cake, a bit like a *clafoutis* in France, but by adding breadcrumbs and using polenta it becomes very much like an Italian bread-and-butter pudding. It's something that Italians would cook in the embers of the fire after dinner.

a dollop of butter
1 cup polenta
1¾ cups all-purpose flour, sifted
2 cups stale breadcrumbs
⅓ cup sugar, plus extra
  for dusting
2¼ cups whole milk
3 large free-range eggs, preferably
  organic, beaten
3 tablespoons honey

¼ cup olive oil
3½ oz. dried figs, chopped or torn up
3½ oz. raisins or sultanas
1 lb. 2 oz. firm eating apples, peeled, cored,
  and roughly diced
½ a teaspoon ground cinnamon
zest of 2 oranges
zest of 2 lemons
1 teaspoon salt

Preheat the oven to 350°F and butter a shallow 11-inch tart tin with a removable bottom. Mix the polenta, flour, breadcrumbs, and sugar in a large bowl. In a separate bowl, mix together the milk, eggs, honey, and olive oil. Add the wet mixture to the dry mixture, making sure you stir it all together well. Add the figs, raisins, apples, cinnamon, orange and lemon zest, and salt, and stir again.

Pour the mixture into your tin and bake for about 50 minutes. Keep an eye on it – you may need to cover it with some aluminum foil if you find that it starts to brown too much at the edges. Before serving, sprinkle some granulated sugar over it. Then make sure you eat it warm – lovely with a dollop of crème fraîche and a glass of vin santo!

torta di riso

florentine rice tart

I just had to put this recipe in the book because it's a real bloody treat to eat! Also, it's not often you come across great portable desserts for picnics or when you're traveling. I first came across small versions of this in a café in Florence, where I saw people buying them. They looked so nice I ordered some for myself – having thought they looked very much like Portuguese custard tarts, I realized they were actually filled with something very similar to a British rice pudding. They were great to eat, but more than that, they really brought home to me how small the food world is. The vanilla- and orange-scented filling can just as easily be eaten alone with a nice glass of dessert wine.

Normally the tarts are dusted with powdered sugar and can be eaten warm or cold – great, like most things in Italy, alongside a coffee. Another good thing to know when you come to make these is that the best results usually come from making the rice pudding the day before.

PS, When you make your pastry for this tart, try using the zest of ½ an orange in place of the lemon zest.

1 shortcrust pastry (see page 279)

for the filling
4 tablespoons unsalted butter
2 vanilla beans
1½ cups risotto rice
3 tablespoons granulated sugar

zest of 3 oranges
1 wineglass of white wine
3½ cups whole milk
2 large free-range eggs, preferably organic, whisked
2 tablespoons powdered sugar

First, using a little of your butter, you will need to grease an 11-inch tart tin with a removable bottom. To make your pastry, follow the instructions on page 279 and place the tart case in the freezer for an hour. Then preheat the oven to 350°F and bake the pastry case for around 12 minutes or until lightly golden. Remove from the oven, place to one side, and turn the heat up to 400°F.

Get yourself an appropriately sized high-sided, thick-bottomed pan with a lid and slowly melt the butter in it. Score down the length of the vanilla beans and remove the seeds by scraping a knife down the inside of each half. (You can pop the beans into your sugar jar to make lovely vanilla sugar.) Add the vanilla seeds to the butter and stir. Continue to cook for 1 minute on a low heat before adding your rice with the sugar and orange zest. Turn the heat up to medium, give it a good stir, and add the wine. Keep stirring until the wine has almost cooked away. Now add the milk little by little. Keep the rice on a slow but constant simmer for about 15 minutes, stirring as often as you can. You want it to still have a bite, as you will be cooking it further in the oven, but you also want it to be quite liquidy. Allow the rice pudding to cool slightly, then mix in the whisked eggs. Pour the rice into your tart case, sprinkle it with powdered sugar, and bake for about 20 minutes, until the pastry is golden. Lovely with créme fraîche, sprinkled with orange zest.

torta di more

blackberry tart

I must have made thousands of these tarts when I worked for Antonio Carluccio at the Neal Street Restaurant in London. We used to make them for the Royal Opera House, and people going to see an opera or ballet would have one as part of the poshest picnics in London, in their boxes up above the stage. I once went along on my day off to see *Swan Lake* and looked up to see all the people in the boxes eating my tarts while I was down with the others in the cheaper seats (eating a tube of fruit pastilles!). Not that I was jealous. I just knew how damn good those tarts were! This is such an easy dessert to make, especially if you have a couple of tart shells in your freezer. You can make it with just about any soft fruit – raspberries, blackberries, strawberries, or blueberries, even lightly cooked gooseberries. You are in for a real treat!

1 shortcrust pastry (see page 279)

for the filling
1 vanilla bean
1 lb. 2 oz. mascarpone
½ cup light cream
3 tablespoons sugar

3 tablespoons grappa or vin santo
3¾ pint blackberries (or other fruit,
  see above)
2 tablespoons blackberry or raspberry jam
a small handful of fresh baby mint leaves

First, using a little butter, you will need to grease an 11-inch tart tin with a removable bottom. To make your pastry, follow the instructions on page 279 and then place the tart case in the freezer for an hour. Preheat the oven to 350°F and bake the pastry case for around 12 minutes or until lightly golden.

To make the filling, split the vanilla bean in half lengthwise and scrape out the seeds by running a knife along the inside of each half. Put the mascarpone, cream, vanilla seeds, sugar, and grappa into a large bowl and whip until shiny. Have a taste – you should have an intensely rich, fluffy, and lightly sweetened cream with a fresh hint of grappa. If you can't get grappa, you can do it without, or add a swig of vin santo instead.

Once the pastry has cooled, get yourself a spatula and add the sweetened cream to the pastry case. Smear it all around so it's reasonably level, then cover it with the berries – place them lightly on the cream, no need to push them in. If you want to be a bit more generous than this, feel free, and if you want to mix your berries, you can do this too. Next, in a small pan, melt down a couple of tablespoons of jam with 3 or 4 tablespoons of water. Stir until it becomes a light syrup, then, using a clean pastry brush, lightly dip and dab the fruit with the jam.

Sprinkle with the baby mint leaves before eating. Great served either as one large tart or as small individual ones. Lovely with your afternoon tea or coffee. Either serve right away or place in the fridge until you're ready to eat it.

semifreddo con cioccolato e riso

chocolate and rice semifreddo

I came up with this recipe on the same day that I made the rice tart (see page 284), and it got me thinking about the way that Italians love and respect rice – whether used in puddings or risottos. If you walk through Florence, or any town in Italy, you'll come across many great *gelaterias* (ice cream parlors). It's quite common to see vanilla and rice ice cream, which I think is absolutely fantastic, and I wanted to have a go at making my own. I mixed the leftover rice pudding with traditional Italian glacé fruits, broken-up pieces of chocolate, and pistachio nuts. I then added it to *semifreddo* (translates as "semi-frozen") – a slightly lighter version of ice cream. Fantastic for dinner parties, as you can make it days in advance.

for the rice pudding
2 tablespoons butter
1 vanilla bean
¾ cup risotto (Arborio) rice
2 tablespoons sugar
2 cups white wine
2½ cups whole milk

for the semifreddo
2 tablespoons sugar

4 large free-range eggs, preferably
  organic, separated
2¼ cups heavy cream
a pinch of salt
5½ oz. candied fruit, chopped up
3½ oz. good-quality bittersweet chocolate
  (70% cocoa solids), bashed up
3½ oz. pistachio nuts, shelled
  and roughly chopped

First put a large earthenware dish (10–12 inches) or individual molds into the freezer to chill. Then get yourself a high-sided, thick-bottomed pan with a lid and slowly melt the butter in it. Score down the length of the vanilla bean and remove the seeds by scraping a knife down the inside of each half. Add the seeds to the butter and stir. Continue to cook for 1 minute before adding your rice with the sugar. Turn the heat up to medium, give it a good stir, and add the wine. Keep stirring until it has almost cooked away. Now add the milk little by little. Keep the rice on a slow but constant simmer for 18 to 20 minutes, stirring as often as you can. Remove from the heat and leave until it's completely cold.

To make the *semifreddo* you need three bowls. In one, whisk up the sugar and egg yolks until pale and creamy. In a second bowl, whip up the cream until you get soft peaks forming. Then in a third bowl whisk the egg whites with a pinch of salt until you get very firm peaks forming.

Now add the cream and the egg whites to the large bowl containing the sugar and egg yolk mixture. All your other flavorings should be added at this point as well, so gently fold in the candied fruit, the chocolate, and the pistachios, plus the cold rice pudding. Working quickly, scoop your rice pudding *semifreddo* into your pre-frozen dish, cover it with plastic wrap, and return it to the freezer – it will take at least 4 hours to freeze until firm. It should be taken out and left in the fridge for a while before you serve it, so it softens. It should be nice and scoopable. Lovely with fresh berries.

fichi secchi
sticky Italian figs

Although this recipe is in the desserts chapter and is probably meant to be eaten after dinner, I've actually had it for breakfast and lunch as well. It is always a treat, so I think it's OK to eat it whenever you want!

Around September in Tuscany there are loads of green and purple figs growing on the trees and you can literally just pick them and eat them then and there. They are sweet and juicy and you can use them in so many different salads (lovely with mozzarella cheese) and with puddings (especially ice cream), but I find if you're going to have them after dinner it's best to pair them with an aged crumbly cheese. (I don't really like eating zingy fruit with cheese, so these figs are perfect.)

One day I had picked so many figs that there were lots left over, so that evening I tore them in half, put them on a little wire rack, and popped them into the oven on the lowest temperature (around 120°F or as low as possible). After 2 hours they were ready, but what you can do is turn the oven off and just let them sit there overnight. Next morning these figs were like the most incredible fruit-gum sweets! I had a few of them with a little honey and ricotta on a slice of toast – what a superb way to start the day. You can throw sticky figs into a stew or stir them into pasta dishes, but the best way to eat them is on their own with some really nice salty pecorino, or a similar cheese, and a glass of vin santo. One of life's great pleasures!

PS, These figs are great in almond tarts and surprisingly amazing with roast chicken and game birds, or chopped up and put in gravies to give wonderful sweetness and spice.

fragole con limone e menta

strawberries with lemon and mint

Put a few strawberries into frozen bowls. Squeeze a little lemon juice over them and add a good sprinkling of sugar, a tiny bit of lemon zest, and a little torn fresh mint. Also really nice with a swig of prosecco or another sparkling wine.

gelato con olio e sale

ice cream with olive oil and sea salt

I was served this dish many years ago and was shocked, but it was bloody gorgeous! It can only be made successfully if you use half-decent vanilla ice cream and the best olive oil you can get your hands on. Put a couple of scoops of vanilla ice cream into your bowls. Drizzle over some very-good-quality extra virgin olive oil, preferably one with a nice grassy, flowery flavor, and sprinkle a tiny pinch of sea salt on top. I can't explain what it's like – you'll just have to try it!

Il Buon Gelato

torta di nada

nada's cake

Nada is the beautiful brains behind the business of my dear friend Luca at Villa Petrolo in Tuscany. If you ever fancy a nice little retreat, they have three or four villas that are rented out all year around. You'll probably end up speaking to Nada when you make your booking. She makes a classic Tuscan grape cake which is really amazing, as you can see from the picture. It's a lovely sponge made with butter and extra virgin olive oil, which gives an unusual light and moist cake – with the sweet gooey grapes, it's such a nice thing to eat.

The grapes that Nada uses in her cake are the small, sweet fragola grapes that are available in Tuscany in September. However, these are not so easy to get hold of in Britain or the States, so I've given the recipe a twist by using fresh blueberries, which are best in the early summer months. This gives the cake the same sort of look as Nada's, and it tastes delicious too.

butter and flour, for preparing the cake pan
4 large eggs, at room temperature
1¼ cups sugar
¾ cup unsalted butter, melted
½ cup extra virgin olive oil
¾ cup milk
1 vanilla bean, seeds removed, or
  1 teaspoon pure vanilla extract

3 cups unbleached all-purpose flour
1½ teaspoons baking powder
a good pinch of sea salt
zest of 2 lemons, grated
zest of 2 oranges, grated
1 lb. 6 oz. fresh blueberries,
  or small sweet red grapes such
  as muscat or fragola

Preheat the oven to 350°F. Generously butter a 9-inch cake pan, line the base with waxed paper, and set aside. Either by hand or in the bowl of an electric mixer fitted with a whisk, beat the eggs and sugar for about 3 minutes, until thick and pale yellow, then add the butter, extra virgin olive oil, milk, and vanilla seeds. (Score down the length of the vanilla beans and remove the seeds by scraping a knife down the inside of each half.) Mix well, then sift in the flour, baking powder, and salt. Add the lemon and orange zest and stir with a wooden spoon until thoroughly blended. Set aside for 10 minutes to allow the flour to absorb the liquid.

Stir about a quarter of your blueberries or grapes into the batter, spoon it into your prepared cake pan, and smooth out the top with a spatula. Place the cake pan in the center of your preheated oven and bake for 15 minutes, then remove it from the oven and scatter the remaining blueberries over the top. Gently push them down into the cake, then return it to the oven for another 30–40 minutes, until the top is a deep golden brown and the cake feels quite firm. Put the pan on a rack to cool. After 10 minutes run a knife along the sides of the pan and turn out your cake.

sorbetto di limone

special lemon sherbet

This is a lemon sherbet, but not one of those boiled sweets you used to have as a kid (bright yellow with bashed-up fizzy sugar in the middle of them). Believe it or not, the sweets came well after the real sherbet. As you know, you have granitas, made from shaved ice, and sorbets, which are smooth, creamless ice creams made from a sugar syrup base. Ice cream itself is an egg-custard-based frozen dessert. Then you have sherbets, which are made by adding a little bit of cream to a sorbet base. By adding the cream in small quantities, you get the effect of fizzing on your tongue, which is where the whole sherbet thing comes from. Sherbets are one of my favorite desserts. You can flavor them in loads of different ways, as long as the fruit has a little bit of an acidic kick. Lemon, lime, pineapple, and grapefruit are my favorites.

I know we take ice cream and frozen desserts for granted now, but a hundred-odd years or so ago, when ice creams were just as famous, some poor workers had to carry ice around all winter long and put it into little ice houses so it could be churned and stored as ice cream or sherbet throughout the summer. It must have involved a lot of time and money, and people must have had to think carefully about good flavors, as they wouldn't have wanted to waste any ice. I guess ice would probably have been seen as the equivalent of champagne and oysters today.

1 cup sugar	zest of 1 lemon
1 cup water	1 heaping tablespoon mascarpone
1 cup lemon juice	

Pre-freeze a shallow 8–10-inch container (I chose to use the little pan in the picture) – this will allow the sherbet to freeze nice and quickly.

Put the sugar and water into a pan and bring to a boil, then turn the heat down and continue to simmer for 5 minutes. Once the liquid is clear and syrupy, remove it from the heat and allow it to cool for 15 minutes, then add the lemon juice and zest. Next, add the mascarpone and stir until totally combined. It's very important that you give it a taste at this point. It all depends on the sourness of your lemons, and it's very hard to give an exact recipe that is going to hit it right on the head – all I can say is that the amount of sugar I have suggested should do the job. If, on the other hand, it's so sour that it makes your face totally curl up, you know you need to add a little more sugar until it softens the lemon juice.

Pour into your pre-frozen dish and return it to the freezer – leave it for at least an hour before you check it. If it has started to freeze, fork it up a bit. Do this maybe every hour or so for the next 3 hours, after which it will be ready to eat. It can now be kept for a couple of days in the freezer, with plastic wrap over the top – any longer and it will start to get ice crystals in it. Always a real treat served on its own in a bowl or glass, but also wicked served with whizzed-up raspberries – like a fresh sauce – poured over the top.

la torta della giovane sara

serves 8

young sara's torte

This is a recipe from a beautiful young Italian girl called Sara who helped us out in the kitchen in Tuscany (our photographer fell in love with her – hence the lovely photo!). It was one she learned from her mother, and I can honestly say that it would never have made it into the book unless it was a cracker. Even though she's a typical youngster in her early twenties, unlike a lot of British or American kids she's been pretty well trained by her mother in the cooking department, and this is a fantastic dessert.

1 cup unsalted butter, melted, plus a little
  for the pan
3¾ cups all-purpose flour
4 eggs, preferably organic

2 cups sugar
zest and juice of 1 lemon
1¼-oz. package active dried yeast
3½ oz. pinenuts

Preheat the oven to 350°F. Butter a 12-inch springform pan and line it with a disc of waxed paper. Sprinkle the waxed paper with a little of the flour. Beat the eggs in a large bowl, then mix the yeast with the melted butter. Add this to the eggs, with the sugar, remaining flour, and the lemon zest and juice. Mix together well and pour into the cake pan. Scatter the pinenuts over the top and bake in the preheated oven for about 40 minutes or until golden.

tiramisù veloce

quick tiramisù

There are lots of different recipes for tiramisù – this one includes my favorite twists on the original and it works really well with those bought ladyfingers. Try it – you'll get fantastic results. The word *tiramisù* translates as "pick-me-up."

15 ladyfingers
1 cup good strong coffee,
  freshly brewed
4 tablespoons sugar
1 lb 2 oz. mascarpone

2 vanilla beans
½ cup vin santo or sweet sherry
zest and juice of 1 orange
3½ oz. best-quality bittersweet chocolate
  (70% cocoa solids)

Get yourself a medium deep bowl or dish about 8–10 inches in diameter and arrange your ladyfingers snugly in layers on top of each other. Sweeten your coffee with 2 tablespoons of the sugar. Pour the coffee over the ladyfingers, making sure the top layer is completely covered – you'll see the coffee being sucked up by the ladyfinger. While that's soaking, put your mascarpone into a bowl and whisk it up with the rest of the sugar.

Score the vanilla beans lengthwise and scrape the seeds out into the bowl of mascarpone, keeping the beans for making vanilla sugar if you want to. Continue whisking and as you do so, drizzle in the vin santo or sherry. You want to get the mixture to a loose, shiny consistency. If it's still too thick you can use a little of the orange juice to loosen it before you squeeze the rest of the juice over the ladyfingers. Smear the vanilla mascarpone over the ladyfingers and either grate all the chocolate over it or make shavings using a knife or a peeler. Sprinkle lightly with a little finely grated orange zest and keep in the fridge until you're ready to serve.

macedonia di frutta all'amalfitana

amalfi style fruit salad

This fruit salad conjures up for me the Italian spirit of making what might possibly be a boring old fruit salad, using everyday produce, a little more interesting and sexy. Make sure you get yourself some nice big oranges, or try using grapefruit instead. You can use your imagination with this one and adapt it to the seasons. As I made this in Italy, wild strawberries were easily available so I used them, but feel free to use normal ones instead.

When it comes to desserts in Italy, very often in a restaurant you'll just be offered a choice between a cake, ice cream, or fruit. The fruit will generally be served in a camp way – things like pineapples or melons cut into boat shapes with the slices pushed either way, almost Chinese in style. I'd be the first person to say that serving sorbet in halved fruit is a bit eighties, but, you know what, on a summer's day when you're at home, some lovely strawberries and nice fresh orange, with a bit of booze and a tiny bit of vanilla sugar, served inside the orange halves, is something really special.

2 nice big oranges, halved, any leaves
  kept on
2 big handfuls of wild strawberries,
  or normal strawberries, quartered

2 teaspoons vanilla sugar or
  granulated sugar
a couple of swigs of grappa or limoncello

Halve the oranges and use a spoon or a grapefruit knife to carefully remove the orange flesh, ensuring the orange half stays intact. Cut up the flesh, getting rid of any pith, and put it into a bowl with the strawberries. If preparing this in advance, the fruit can go into the fridge until you're ready to eat it. Just before serving, sprinkle with the vanilla sugar (adjusting the amount according to the sweetness of the fruit) and add a little swig of booze to lift it up a bit – I use grappa or limoncello. Give the fruit a couple of tosses to mix it together, and spoon the fruit and juice back into your halved oranges. Serve straight away.

grazie mille!

Thanks a million to all the lovely people that helped in putting this book together.

Thanks to my beautiful wife, Jools, and my two beautiful girls, Poppy and Daisy, for being a constant source of inspiration. Love you. Thanks to Mum and Dad for conceiving me at the end of Southend Pier thirty years ago.

Wanting to get as much into the book as possible I worked well beyond the normal, acceptable deadlines and I'm sure I drove everyone at Penguin mad, so thanks for putting up with me. Big love and respect to John Hamilton, Tom Weldon, Annie Lee, Keith Taylor, Chris Callard, Sophie Hewat, Tiina Wastie, Sophie Brewer, Alex Clarke, Jessica Jefferys, Rob Williams, Tora Orde-Powlett, Naomi Fidler, and all the sales team, Clare Pollock, Jane Opoku, Mariateresa Boffo (thanks for all the translating!), Jen Doyle, and Sarah Hulbert. You're all brilliant. Who would have thought ten years ago that we'd be on a sixth book?

Massive hugs, kisses, and respect to my own personal team who I feel so happy and completely honored to work with on a daily basis. You all work incredibly hard for me on all my projects with such passion and high standards – the lovely Lindsey Evans, the lovely Ginny Rolfe, cleanest meanest Peter Begg, Anna Jones, Bobby Thomson, Danny McCubbin, Louise Holland, Carly Skinner, Paul Rutherford, and Suzanna de Jong. Thanks guys, you've helped me to get this book together under really tough time constraints xxx (There are bound to be others that I've forgotten . . . so this is to all of you!) Thanks also to the "guvnors" – Frosty, Tara, and Tessa.

Respect and thanks to David Loftus, the photographer – I think this is your best work to date. And Chris Terry for his wonderful additional portraits. Thanks guys, it was worth all the hard work!

Thanks to my mate Jekka McVicar, who sorted out the herbs for my garden and camper van – you should order some seeds or plants from her Web site, www.jekkasherbfarm.com. Thanks to Mick Peart, the one-man band who made the kitchen trailer for my camper van as well as making the world's best barbecues, Caribbean Cookers (www.caribbeancookers.com). And to Marco from Illy Coffee UK. He supported the Fifteen restaurant from day one and has now started to import incredible veg seeds from Italy to sell by mail order – www.seedsofitaly.com. Also thanks to Gretchen Andersen, Ewan and Agnes at the Lacquer Chest and to Anna Brown for additional translating.

Thanks to my main men Luke, Peter, Paul, and Carl for helping out with my 1956 VW split-screen camper, which did very well but it did break down a couple of times. Without you a chunk of this book would not have been written as I'd never have made it to where I was going. And flying out to Italy with a gearbox in your suitcase is bloody good service! Thanks to Luc and Mark and all the gang at Tefal for shipping some beautiful pans out to me in the middle of Italy when I needed some.

To my best friend and professional ponce, Andy Slade the gasman – without you my life wouldn't be complete, you raving idiot! Thanks for leaving me long, drunken midnight messages on my phone to remind me of all my friends back home that I was missing on my trip.

I'd also like to thank my production crew who, in some unusual and odd situations, really helped me to find and capture some amazing, undiscovered parts of Italy – Andrew Conrad, Robert Thirkell, Helen Simpson, Guy Gilbert, Katy Fryer, Victoria Bennetts, Benedict Protheroe, Carla de Nicola, Sarah Tildesley, Toby Ralph, Richard Munns, Tracy Garrett, Vanya Barwell, Tom Dalzell, Paolo Chianta, Guendalina Ghironi, Emma Cockshutt, John Dewar, Sabrina Licata, Sunshine Jackson, and Paddy Lynas.

Last but not least, thanks to all the incredible people that I met on my trip around Italy, of which there are too many of you to thank separately. Big love and thank you for your kindness.

index **317**